10657522

ALISON HARDINGHAM grew up in Malvern, Worcestershire, and studied psychology at Lady Margaret Hall, Oxford. She trained as a teacher and worked in teaching before moving on to educational psychology, including family therapy and assessment of children. She now works as a business psychologist, in the area of management assessment and training. She has particular expertise in the assessment of an individual's strengths and development needs in relation to his or her chosen career. Alison's first book was *How to Make Successful Decisions* (Sheldon 1988).

Overcoming Common Problems Series

The ABC of Eating
Coping with anorexia, bulimia and
compulsive eating
JOY MELVILLE

Beating the Blues
SUSAN TANNER AND JILLIAN
BALL

Beating Job Burnout
DR DONALD SCOTT

Being the Boss
STEPHEN FITZSIMON

Birth Over Thirty
SHEILA KITZINGER

Body Language
How to read others' thoughts by their
gestures
ALLAN PEASE

Bodypower
DR VERNON COLEMAN

Calm Down
How to cope with frustration and anger
DR PAUL HAUCK

Comfort for Depression
JANET HORWOOD

Common Childhood Illnesses
DR PATRICIA GILBERT

Complete Public Speaker
GYLES BRANDRETH

Coping with Anxiety and Depression
SHIRLEY TRICKETT

Coping with Depression and Elation
DR PATRICK McKEON

Coping with Stress
DR GEORGIA WITKIN-LANOIL

Coping with Suicide
DR DONALD SCOTT

Coping with Thrush
CAROLINE CLAYTON

**Coping Successfully with Your Child's
Asthma**
DR PAUL CARSON

**Coping Successfully with Your Child's Skin
Problems**
DR PAUL CARSON

**Coping Successfully with Your Hyperactive
Child**
DR PAUL CARSON

Coping Successfully with Your Irritable Bowel
ROSEMARY NICOL

Curing Arthritis Diet Book
MARGARET HILLS

Curing Arthritis – The Drug-free Way
MARGARET HILLS

**Curing Coughs, Colds and Flu – the
Drug-free Way**
MARGARET HILLS

Curing Illness – The Drug-free Way
MARGARET HILLS

Depression
DR PAUL HAUCK

Divorce and Separation
ANGELA WILLANS

The Dr Moerman Cancer Diet
RUTH JOCHEMS

The Epilepsy Handbook
SHELAGH McGOVERN

**Everything You Need to Know about
Adoption**
MAGGIE JONES

**Everything You Need to Know about
Contact Lenses**
DR ROBERT YOUNGSON

**Everything You Need to Know about Your
Eyes**
DR ROBERT YOUNGSON

**Everything You Need to Know about the
Pill**
WENDY COOPER AND TOM SMITH

Everything You Need to Know about Shingles
DR ROBERT YOUNGSON

Family First Aid and Emergency Handbook
DR ANDREW STANWAY

Overcoming Common Problems Series

Overcoming Common Problems Series

HOW TO GET THINGS DONE

Alison Hardingham

SHELDON PRESS
LONDON

First published in Great Britain 1990
Sheldon Press, SPCK, Marylebone Road, London NW1 4DU

© Alison Hardingham 1990

British Library Cataloguing in Publication Data
Hardingham, Alison
    How to get things done. – (Overcoming common problems)
    1. Man. Achievement motivation
    I. Title   II. Series
    153.8

    ISBN 0–85969–605–7

Photoset by Deltatype Ltd, Ellesmere Port, Cheshire
Printed in Great Britain by Courier International Ltd, Tiptree, Essex

Contents

Introduction

All of us get a great many things done, every day, without thinking much about our achievement or expecting any recognition. If any one of us were to sit down and write a list of everything we had brought about during that day, we should no doubt be surprised at the length and variety of that list. It might include things we do for ourselves and things we do for other people, or things we persuaded, instructed, or paid someone else to do. There is no doubt about it: each one of us is a great and continuous achiever. Yet it is just as true that for all of us there are many things we meant to do but never got round to. We say to one another: 'There aren't enough hours in the day' or 'I never seem to achieve anything.' Often we are busy for days, yet feel we have accomplished nothing – and for many of us there is a sense of unrealized potential and maybe even real frustration.

This book is about overcoming frustration and realizing potential. It is about how to get things done. Its objective is to enable you to achieve those goals you have always wanted to achieve, without requiring you to drop all the other activities that currently fill your life. It is about finding extra time and making better use of all your time. It is about becoming, and feeling, more effective.

The book is divided into two parts. The first part deals with getting things done yourself. It discusses how we are often our own worst enemies, and outlines a five-point plan for changing that. It won't turn you into Superman (or Superwoman), but it will enable you to make the best use of the talents and energy you already possess.

The second part of the book deals with getting other people to do things. It covers both paying people to do things and, even more tricky, persuading people to do things. It includes getting your husband, your children, your neighbour, the builders and the garage to do things. It provides advice on, among other things, how to be clear about what you want without being bossy, how you can cope with embarrassment about paying people, and how you can make sure that people do what you asked them to do.

It doesn't really matter what it is you want to get done. This book will even help you work out what you want if you don't know yet. You might simply want to spend more time with your children; you might want to learn to fly a plane; you might want to paint watercolours, revise for exams, find a new job, or write a book! But one thing is certain: you want to get more done, better.

This book is mainly about getting things done at home, in your own time. There are lots of books on how to get more done at work, and many aimed specifically at managers. Yet it is just as important for most of us to use our own time effectively. So this book is in response to that gap, and it draws most of its examples from everyday life. Everything in it is relevant to getting things done at work, but there are some important aspects to getting things done at work which are not dealt with here (for example, office politics, matching your commitment to your employer's investment, and so on).

Getting things done makes us feel confident. The more confident we feel, the more we can get done. This book should start you off on this truly virtuous circle.

PART ONE

How to Get Things Done Yourself

1

Why Things Don't Get Done

Reasons and excuses

There are always plenty of 'good' reasons why things don't get done. Have you ever tried to reprove someone for not doing something? Imagine asking your teenage daughter, accusingly, why she hasn't done her homework, or your secretary why she hasn't typed that letter yet, or the electricity board why they haven't read your meter for over six months.

You will have no difficulty in also imagining the flood of plausible reasons you will be given. The homework wasn't important/could be done on the bus tomorrow/wasn't clearly specified. The letter had to take its place in a backlog of work/the secretarial department is short-staffed at the moment/your secretary didn't realize it was urgent. You weren't in when the electricity man came/the board has forgotten where your meter is/there has been a computer error.

It is almost impossible to discover the 'real' reasons, to tell the reasons from the excuses. Not only that, it is often futile. The minute someone is put on the defensive about their failure to get something done, the truth about how or why they didn't do it flies out of the window. All they are interested in doing is justifying themselves. The road to really understanding why something has not been done is blocked.

The same pattern often prevents us asking ourselves why we haven't got things done. The very idea makes us feel defensive. Of course we haven't painted the bathroom yet: when have we had the time? Naturally we haven't written that letter: how could we until we had confirmed our holiday dates? One of the things that makes it very difficult for us to get more done, to change into a higher gear, is that we have a complex web of self-justification and rationalization bolstering our existing pattern of achievement.

Yet if we want to start getting more done, we need to be able to consider why we haven't achieved enough in the past so that we can change. So we must set our defensiveness on one side and be honest with ourselves. We must recognize when our reasons are merely excuses, and in fact unrelated to our failure to get something done.

5

What follows in this chapter is a series of fundamental reasons why things don't get done. Some will apply to you; some will not. But in order to be able to judge whether they do or not, you must keep this thought at the front of your mind, 'I am not under attack. This exercise is not about how much I have failed, but about how I could do even more.'

Time

The single most commonly quoted reason for not doing something is the lack of time. Yet since we all have at our disposal approximately the same number of hours a day, time cannot account for the enormous variation in the amount different people achieve. Give one person an hour and he will walk the dog, do the shopping and telephone three people. Give another person an hour, and he will let the time slip by with nothing achieved. Lack of time is not in itself why most of us don't get more done.

Inability to manage time effectively is a much more likely candidate as a genuine reason for not getting things done. Later chapters discuss how you can manage time better if you think this is your problem.

If you're not sure whether managing time is your problem or not, quickly answer the following ten questions with a simple 'yes' or 'no'.

1. Do you often get to the end of a day having done little of what you intended to do, and feeling unsure what you did instead?
2. Do deadlines frighten you?
3. Do you often forget what you were going to do?
4. Are you often in a rush?
5. Do you seldom have time to relax?
6. Are you often late for appointments?
7. Do you often have to apologize to other people because you haven't done what you said you would?
8. Would you say other people generally 'work faster' than you?
9. Can you immediately call to mind a whole string of things you should have done this week but haven't?
10. Are you often surprised by how much other people get done in a day?

If you answered 'yes' to any of these questions, your ability to manage time effectively could do with a bit of attention. If you answered 'yes' to five or more, then you have a serious problem! Chapter 2 will help you solve it.

Money

There are quite a lot of things which cannot be done without money. Decorating a room requires paint; applying for jobs requires stamps for letters and good writing paper; at the other end of the scale, starting a business usually requires capital investment. So some schemes do have to be abandoned for lack of funds.

Purely financial hurdles can often be overcome, however. There are usually several ways of going about things, some more expensive than others. Designing and constructing a small garden is an example of something which can cost anything from tens to thousands of pounds. Also, for most of us, there are usually at any time several things we should like to get done, so if we haven't much spare cash, we can just choose one which doesn't require any financial outlay. Some of our new activities may even generate some cash to fund others – I have known people earn money through casual activities such as selling cakes and pies in the local delicatessen, decorating other people's houses, making and selling Christmas cards, looking after children, tutoring; and of course the better you become at getting things done, the more possible such activities will be.

The elasticity of time and money

Time and money are often classed together as the all-important limiting factors on what we can achieve. Yet, as I have hinted already, I think both time and money are more remarkable for their *elasticity* than their *resistance*. They contract and stretch in apparently inexplicable ways; in different people's hands, they behave totally differently. The spendthrift 'cannot get by' on an income of hundreds of thousands of pounds a year; others manage to save money on an income of only a few thousand pounds.

If you have ever been involved in a car accident you will know that strange sensation of the passage of events slowing down, when you experience minutes worth of thoughts and feelings telescoped into a couple of seconds. And of course when you fall asleep hours pass 'in no time at all'.

There is enormous potential in the elasticity of time and money, potential for us to control and for us to achieve what we want to, in the time we have available, with whatever resources are at our disposal.

But to get control of this potential, we must investigate some of what I would call the *real* reasons why things don't get done.

Lack of 'application'

To get even trivial things done requires a certain amount of single-mindedness. Imagine trying to change a plug, or cook a meal, while dictating a letter apologizing for forgetting your aunt's birthday. You wouldn't be able to do it, not because your hands weren't free, but because your *mind* wasn't free enough. Some actions are completely reflex, so we don't have to think about them at all (breathing, blinking, for example, and for many of us driving along a straight empty road in a familiar car). But most require a fair amount of our attention and many require all of it. Psychologists have a longstanding debate about whether it is even possible to pay attention to more than two things at once, or whether we only appear to do so by switching our attention rapidly between one activity and another. Whatever the truth about this is, divided attention means things don't get done.

So when people say – 'He'll never do it. He doesn't apply himself' – what they really mean is that he applies himself to too many things at once. And very commonly such a person is constantly distracted by some thing or things in his life he doesn't actually want to think about at all, to the detriment of things he does want to think about.

The classic case of this is the man whose work goes to pieces because his marriage is breaking up. He can't apply himself to his work because his mind, and his energies, keep drifting into his anxiety over his marriage.

This is an extreme example. But the pattern is a common one. It is found in the schoolgrl who does badly with her homework because she's infatuated with the boy next door, and the housewife who rushes round the house partly cleaning every room because her mind is already on the next job. It is found in all of us at some time or another.

There are all sorts of reasons behind 'lack of application', all sorts of things which distract us and sap our energies. Correspondingly,

8

there are lots of ways of putting ourselves back in charge of our attention and directing it, singlemindedly, where we want it to go. Chapters 3 and 4 explore some of these.

Fear of failure

If you never attempt anything, you won't ever fail at anything. And failure is much more frightening to most of us than simple mediocrity. After all, we can always tell ourselves that if we ever *really* wanted to/needed to/had to, we could do it. We don't put this assertion to the test, and of course the longer we have been saying this to ourselves (and maybe to other people) the more risky it would be to put it to the test.

Why is it that some of us are so frightened of failure? Fear of failure is by no means most commonly found in the incompetent. In fact, it is very often found in very clever or gifted people. Sometimes it is the factor which drives them on, makes them scale higher and higher mountains, still terrified no matter how high they climb, that the abominable snowman of failure will catch up with them and drag them by the heels into the abyss.

In this book, however, we are concerned with those who are frozen, rather than driven, by their fear of failure.

It is probable that a strong fear of failure starts in childhood. Its origins can be found in early experiences of failure being disastrous and, just as potently, in being surrounded as a child by people who believed failure would be disastrous. This belief can be expressed by parents in two quite different but equally destructive ways. They may either punish failure inappropriately harshly, because their own anxiety about it makes them unable to tolerate it in the family. Or they may so cosset and protect their child that he is never allowed to experience failure. Everything he does or doesn't do is defined as good, right, successful, and so he grows up never having learnt to cope with failure and dimly conscious that it must be awful indeed.

In this book we shall be looking at how inappropriate it is in most important things in life to talk about absolute success or failure. We shall be working out ways of overcoming fear of failure, and of making disastrous failure extremely unlikely. Most of us are a little bit frightened of failing, and of course if we didn't care we wouldn't bother and so probably wouldn't achieve anything anyway. But we have to get the balance between fear and confidence right, to get started.

Fear of success

Fear of success is a strange idea, when you first come across it, and yet it is certainly widespread. Success can separate you from the crowd, isolate you, and generate its own demands. How much easier it is just to be ordinary!

You only have to look at pop stars to see how dangerous success can be. Probably one of the reasons we like reading about their unhappy, traumatic lives is that such stories reassure us that we are much better off living quietly, not excelling.

Even on a smaller scale, fear of success exerts its insidious influence. Many children underachieve because they don't want to be called 'teacher's pet'. Belonging is more important to most of us than standing out, and from an early age we learn how to match our achievements to the norm.

This was tragically illustrated in the story of a friend's brother. He was a brilliant mathematician. At school he was exceptional. People were rather in awe of him, and of course he realized it. He wasn't disliked, in fact people generally admired him, but his intelligence separated him from his peers. When he won a scholarship to Oxford University, he was very pleased. He imagined that Oxford would be a place where there were lots of brilliant mathematicians like him, and at last he would belong. When he went up to Oxford, and discovered he was exceptional even there, he became desperately unhappy, eventually committing suicide.

Part of the secret of getting things done is wanting to achieve things for yourself. Always looking behind you and around you, always thinking about what others will think and whether something will be acceptable to the rest of the world or not, this will sap your determination and stop you getting things done. Fear of success has to be put to one side. Because if you underachieve in order to belong, you aren't really belonging. You have sacrificed yourself in order to conform, and given up for ever the chance of being yourself with other people.

Success doesn't close doors, it opens them. Some of the happiest people are those who have experienced a great deal of success, and handled it on their terms. Often they have needed good friends, a supportive husband, a loving family to do this. But they haven't run away from their potential. That way lies vague discontent, frustration, and immense loss. The best motto to combat fear of success is

'Go for it. And when you've got it, that's the time to work out how to handle it.'

You might think this discussion of fear of success is a long way removed from your inability to get the housework done, or manage a part-time job. But before you dismiss the idea, ask yourself how your friends and family would react if you started getting these things done. Do you imagine they would be surprised and pleased? If so you're probably not afraid of success. Or do you imagine they would be put out, annoyed? You wouldn't be the comfortable muddler they're used to. You might even be a bit threatening. If you think they might react like that, fear of success could be a problem for you.

Other people's expectations

'No man is an island,' John Donne said, and this has profound consequences for our ability to get things done. Each one of us is a part of several semipermanent and permanent social groups, such as our family of origin (the family we were born into), our created family (the family we are creating ourselves), work organization, local community, and various clubs. We can call these social groups 'systems'. In each of these systems we have a role, which complements and is sustained by the role of other people in the system.

In an office, for example, you typically find a 'sympathetic listener', a 'moody' person, a 'lame duck', and so on. As soon as you have a role in a group, it is very difficult to step outside its narrow confines. Imagine the 'lame duck' trying to take charge of the office social club.

So if your role in one or more of the important systems you are part of doesn't allow you to get things done in general, or one thing done in particular, you will have to fight the system to do it. Many families, for example, recognize only one high achiever in their midst; it is very difficult for anyone else in the family to borrow some of that role. Even when they do achieve things, this is seen as somehow exceptional or unusual, and this attitude undermines their belief that they might make a habit of achieving things.

It is very hard, although not impossible, to change other people's expectations. Sometimes the only way to get started is to avoid them rather than change them. In Chapter 5 we investigate how you do this.

Worry

Worry is a colossal time-waster, next to guilt (of which more in Chapter 4) the most useless powerful feeling we experience. One of the teachers at my grammar school who had a great influence over me once gave us a rare opportunity to talk about our hopes and fears. 'A' levels were close at hand, and we were all pretty neurotic. One of us asked her what we could do when we couldn't get to sleep for worrying about our exams. She replied, much to our dismay at the time, that we should get out of bed and do some revision.

This comment has stayed with me as one of the most profound I ever heard at school. No amount of thinking will cure worry. But getting something done in spite of it *might*.

Aiming too high

Please answer the following questions:

1. Have you ever had a research paper of major scientific importance published?
2. Have you ever appeared in a film?
3. Do you run your home completely single-handed and keep it spotlessly clean from top to bottom?
4. Are all your children exceptionally bright, unusually popular and saintly in their dispositions?
5. Have you helped every single human being in need that has ever crossed your path?

Now, how do you feel? Pretty despondent and underachieving, I should imagine.

Now answer *these* questions:

1. Have you been kind to someone recently?
2. Have you cooked a nice meal during the last few days?
3. Have you tidied up a room or organized some paperwork in the last week?
4. Have you written a letter to a friend or relative recently?
5. Have you arranged something for a member of your family today?

Do you feel better? I hope so!

Believe it or not, the first set of questions represents the kinds of targets many of us carry around in our heads. Small wonder we feel we don't get anything done (and small wonder we don't often get any of *these* done).

If we aim too high we disappoint ourselves and become despondent. There is simply no point in aiming to become the first woman President of the United States.

Apart from these extremes, which are recognizable to all of us in our sane moments as unreasonable, many of us aim too high for ourselves, at the moment. Suppose your husband has just left you. Don't aim to get started on a new lucrative career right away. It's too much to expect; you'll fail, and be more despondent than before. Just aim to get a part-time job, for the moment.

Chapter 2 looks more closely at how we can set achievement targets.

The entropy of the universe

The entropy of the universe is not a reason why *you* don't get things done. It is the backcloth to all our efforts to achieve. It is important to understand that the natural progression of things is towards chaos. It takes nearly all our energy just to maintain the order that is there, or to impose a bit of extra order.

And that is what getting things done is all about. That is why we should congratulate ourselves when we get just a tiny thing done, like the washing-up or filling the car up with petrol. We are working against the grain all the time. So we need reserves of energy, physical, mental, and spiritual. Chapters 3 and 4 provide insight into how we access those reserves.

2

A Five-point Plan for Getting Things Done

Introduction to the plan

The fact that we are going to talk in terms of a 'five-point plan' is in itself an example of two of the cardinal principles of getting things done. First of these is the importance of a plan of campaign. As soon as we formulate a plan, we are transferred from murky chaos onto a highway. The very act of having a plan gives us confidence and determination. No matter if we never actually carry out *this plan*; leaders of military campaigns have since the beginning of conflict recognized the strength and resolve that are imparted to troops by even the most superficial of plans.

The second cardinal principle, which we have already mentioned in Chapter 1, and which will come up again and again, is that of setting achievable targets. So we are not about to embark on a 100-point plan, or even a ten-point plan, but a nice manageable five-point plan.

This plan is shown in the box below. From now on, it will be referred to as the KR–3W plan – from the first letter of each point.

The five-point plan for getting things done
1. Know your strengths
2. Recognize your limitations
3. Work out why
4. Work out when
5. Work out how
   'KR–3W'

It starts, as does all personal development, with learning more about yourself. *You* are your major resource for getting things done, and you need to know your strengths and limitations, plus-points and minus-points, hopes and fears, as well as you possibly can. After all, if you were put in charge of someone else, a secretary, a nanny, a

14

junior colleague, you would make sure you found out about them before you gave them anything to do. And of course, none of us can assume we 'already know' our strengths and weaknesses. When did you last really look at them?

Points 3, 4 and 5 of the KR–3W plan, the 3 Ws, (work out why, work out when and work out how), are to do with designing the best approach for the task in hand. That is when you place yourself, with your known strengths and weaknesses, on one side of the scales, and the task on the other, and attempt to balance the scales, to match your resources to your objective.

The KR–3W plan gets us started. Chapter 5 discusses how we keep going.

Know your strengths

It makes sense to invest most of your time doing things you are good at. (You see that I assume we are all good at some things. This assumption is well-founded. Increasingly the evidence, from the world of work and from research into personality characteristics, is that, first, no-one is good at everything, and second, everyone has areas of strength and areas of weakness.) Of course sometimes we have to do some things we consider ourselves bad at: I have to make my face up every weekday morning, for example, even though I don't think I'm very good at it. A friend of mine has to cook for her family every evening though she dislikes cooking and has little flair for it. But then one day perhaps her husband, or one of her children, will become proficient at cooking, and then no doubt she will drop that particular duty like a hot brick and leave the stove for ever, to decorate the house, mend things, and organize the family finances, all of which she does rather well.

The point I am trying to make is that you need to know your strengths so that when you do have the choice you try to get the right things done, the things that you are most likely to succeed at, most quickly.

Psychologists have a range of questionnaires which they can ask people to fill in to discover their strengths and weaknesses. Career guidance people do similar things. It is often just as useful, though, simply to sit down and write a list of things you think you are good at. Here is a sample list, to get you started. Put the following in order, with the one you are best at first, and the one you are worst at last.

Cooking
Dressmaking
Gardening
Mending the car
Reading aloud
Budgeting
Do-it-yourself
Writing letters
Supermarket shopping
Talking (!)
Listening

Most of us find it extremely difficult to think of our strengths, to know our good points, our skills and our talents. There is something about our system of education and about the way we are brought up which makes us think that it's somehow not 'nice' to dwell on what we have to offer. I suppose we believe it might lead to bigheadedness and conceit – and we have all received plenty of dire warnings about pride coming before a fall and nobody liking bigheads. Yet if we don't know what we have to offer, we may well shortchange the people around us – and, more importantly, I believe, ourselves. The important thing in understanding our own strengths is remembering that everyone else has strengths too. Then we won't become conceited because we will know that we are *good* but not *better*.

Anyway, since it is so difficult for us to list our good points, here are a few more ideas to get you started.

1. Think of someone you like, respect or admire. It is better if it is someone you actually know, rather than a famous personality or someone from history. Make a list of their strengths, but every time you write a strength down for them, write one down for yourself. Somehow, praising someone else makes praising yourself a little easier.
2. Think of times when you have received praise or thanks from other people. What did you do? Does a pattern begin to emerge?

(For example, are you often thanked for mending things, or for being patient?)

It is worth mentioning here that in general we are not very good at praising each other. So if you can't think of any examples, don't imagine it's because you never do anything worthwhile!

3. Think of things you criticize others for. It may be that you don't voice criticism, but you think to yourself, 'I could do better'. Well, maybe you could!

4. What do you like doing most? We are often best at the things we enjoy.

5. Here is a list of pairs of opposites. For each pair, tick the one you think you are *better* at. This process, known as 'forced choice' because it forces you to choose one or the other, will suggest to you your relative strengths. (By the way, this list of opposites is in no particular order and is certainly not comprehensive. There is an infinite number of strengths you might have!)

Being practical	Being imaginative
Completing things I've started	Having ideas for new things
Doing things on my own	Doing things with others
Planning and organizing	Doing things on the spur of the moment
Measuring precisely	Estimating
Writing	Talking
Telling	Listening
Giving people clear instructions	Telling stories
Performing in front of others	Getting on with things quietly
Getting things done in a rush	Being painstaking
Tackling big jobs	Paying attention to details

17

Waiting	Acting immediately
Being in charge	Following instructions
Putting up with discomfort	Thinking of ways to make tasks pleasanter

You can see from this list how many different kinds of strength there are which you might have. We often define 'strength' too narrowly – maybe in terms of being good at academic subjects, sporty or practical. Our understanding of what a strength is may still be based on school definitions of 'subjects'. Yet in adult life many skills and attributes are potentially important: in fact, it is now widely acknowledged that career success has far more to do with general characteristics like ability to communicate well with people and work hard than with excellence in any particular subject area.

So cast your net wide as you examine your strengths – you might not rate very highly your ability to walk for miles while shopping, but it suggests stamina and determination, which should be key qualities on anyone's list!

So far, we have been thinking about 'strengths' in terms of 'activities we are good at'. However, other aspects are important, such as what time of day you're most energetic, whether you work best under pressure, and so on. These aspects will be dealt with in Chapter 4.

Recognize your limitations

Perhaps it seems rather negative to talk of recognizing limitations. After all, don't some philosophies teach 'Anything you want to do, you can do'? And it would be depressing to dwell on our shortcomings.

In fact, what I mean by 'recognize your limitations' does need some qualification. I am not using the word 'limitation' in the sense of immovable characteristics fixed for ever. I don't believe in those kinds of limitations. I am talking about limitations which arise from where you are, who you are, what you are, at a particular point in time and space. Your limitations will change from day to day, week to week, year to year. If you are understanding your potential right, your limitations will be different every time you look.

18

Understanding that limitations are temporary is the difference between saying 'I can't set up my own business now' and 'I shall never be able to set up my own business.' The step of recognizing limitations and setting your targets in the light of them is particularly important for those whose main block to attempting is fear of failure. Those people need to avoid failure, especially in the early stages, or they will give up for good.

Although limitations are temporary, they are important. Unless we recognize them, we shall often be trying to achieve something in the wrong place or at the wrong time. If you've just changed jobs, for example, now is not the time to take on major new commitments at home. Either your new job will suffer or the new commitments will. If you've just suffered a major drop in income, now is not the time to start building an extension to your house.

I wonder if you know the type of person who almost seems to attempt too much on purpose, who dashes from crisis to crisis, creating panic in those around him. He certainly fails to recognize his limitations. I suspect that some people who behave in this way attempt too much to avoid being blamed for not achieving. After all, you can hardly ever hold them still long enough for a conversation, let alone for a rational analysis of what they are attempting and whether they are going to succeed. (Their problem, in the terms we discussed in Chapter 1, is 'aiming too high'.)

Of course it takes courage to admit, even if only for the time being, that there are things we cannot do. I find it extremely difficult ever to refuse an assignment at work, even when there is no external pressure on me to do it at all and when it is totally impossible to do it in the time available. I think we all have a tendency to categorize people into just *two* boxes – those who can and those who can't. We are terrified that if we say we can't even once, we will slip from the 'can' box into the 'can't' box. Each of us has different areas where we can't say no. A very good friend of mine can't say no to her children – she's afraid of falling into the 'bad mother' box. Another acquaintance can't say no to a social invitation – she's afraid of falling into the 'never-goes-out' box.

What we all need to recognize is that these simple black and white characteristics are totally inappropriate. Today we can do this, tomorrow that, the day after maybe both but not something else. The way to getting one thing done *requires* us to leave other things undone.

19

So how can we set achievable targets, that will allow us to get done those things we can get done and put to one side those things that we can't get done at this point in time?

The first thing is to make your targets clear. Suppose you want to get a new job. 'Getting a new job' isn't a clear enough target to get you going and see you through. It contains a mixture of things, some of which you have control over, some of which you don't. Suppose you live in an area of high unemployment and you are not very mobile. You may fail to get a new job through no fault of your own.

So, often targets need to be broken down a bit, into smaller targets, which are in your power to achieve. 'Getting a new job' might break down into the following:

- Writing an up-to-date CV.
- Getting it typed up, and asking a good friend to review it to check it makes the most of you.
- Looking in the papers every day for jobs.
- Sending the CV off to at least six possibles, together with carefully written letters.

Here at last are some targets you can achieve! And your sense of achievement and confidence will grow as you successfully complete each step – a very useful preparation for interviews!

Let us take another example. Suppose you are feeling stressed at work. You sense resentment in the people working for you, and deadlines are failing to be met. You decide that you need to change your management style. (If you are interested in the process by which you can reach a sound decision in situations like this, you might like to read my previous book, *How to Make Successful Decisions*.) Now, 'change my management style' is too broad and vague a target. It needs to be broken down in a big way. Here are some of the subtargets which might drop out:

- Spending at least half an hour a week with each person who works for you, discussing how the work is going.
- Leaving the door to your office open.
- Returning all work submitted to you for review within a week maximum.

- Asking people to take it in turns to chair your monthly progress meetings.

Here is a final example. Suppose you want to 'decorate the house'. (This is just the kind of general goal guaranteed to produce paralysis in all but the most stouthearted.) Obvious ways of breaking this target down are room by room – but be careful that you allow yourself the time and opportunity to congratulate yourself as each room gets done. It is surprising how often when people begin to achieve they dwell on how much farther there is to go rather than on what they have accomplished already, and in this sense although their targets may appear achievable the 'real' targets they are working to are ridiculously ambitious.

Work out why

The third step in the KR–3W five-point plan has to do with motivation. Understood literally, to 'motivate' is to 'move or bring forward'. Unless you are motivated, you are likely to be stuck, however hard you work. Unless you understand what you are working towards, why you are trying to get a particular thing done, you will waste time and effort diverting into side paths and, more importantly, it is extremely unlikely you will be able to keep going.

For examples of what happens when people embark on activities without understanding the point of them, we only have to look at our education system. For many children, what is studied at school seems arbitrary and useless. They haven't the faintest idea why they should learn algebra, grammar or about the Kings and Queens of England. It all seems far removed from anything that matters to them, and only vaguely connected with getting a job. They know they need to pass exams, but they don't really understand why, and they certainly don't understand why these exams need to test such peculiar skills and knowledge. So many of them lack motivation and underachieve. They have to be forced to do the work by threats of punishment. They have to be 'disciplined' and appear to have no self-discipline of their own.

Yet many of them will work long hard hours to mend a bike, earn money on Saturdays, or help with handicapped children. In a context where they understand why they are working they show enormous self-discipline.

As adults, we don't have the equivalent of teachers to force us to get things done when our motivation is lacking. So it is even more important for us to understand why we are doing something.

Let's look at an example of the kind of self-questioning you should engage in before you commit yourself to a task, the kinds of answers you might come up with and what they imply for how effectively you will get the task done.

I'm going to dig a new flowerbed in the lawn.

Why?

Answer 1. I've seen one next door and it looked good. [Be careful: will it suit your garden? Aren't there other things which would improve your garden as much and take less time? You might waste time, or lose heart.]

Answer 2. I want the opportunity to grow some new flowers and the rest of the borders are full. [Sounds like a good reason – you're already thinking about the new opportunities that successful accomplishment of the task will create.]

Answer 3. My husband has asked me to. [Well, the likelihood of your getting this done depends on how much you like doing what you're told by your husband! Not a very good start.]

Answer 4. The garden looks a mess. [So will a new flowerbed really improve things? Take care: you might waste time, or lose heart.]

Time spent asking 'why?' is never wasted. Only by doing so can we work out whether what we're planning will really get us where we want to be. And I would hazard that the things we stand most chance of getting done successfully are those things where we know very definitely why we are doing them.

Also, it is important, for your wellbeing and sense of personal effectiveness, to keep a balance between things you do for other people and things you do for yourself. Asking why enables you to find out which category each planned activity falls into.

The final, but very important, point to be made is that when you ask why you suddenly realize that many things you thought you had to do aren't really necessary at all. I often use this technique to prevent myself buying things which have caught my eye, but it is just as useful in preventing us wasting time on pointless activities. 'I must clean the car.' Why? Take it through the carwash next time you're in the garage. 'I must go shopping.' Why? You can make do with what's in the larder. 'I must reorganize our filing system.' Must you? It's a wonderfully easy way of expanding time, simply relegating some of the activities you were about to embark on without thinking to the non-essential category.

Motivation is what gets us going in the first place and what keeps us going. There are routine tasks, such as paperwork, cleaning, and servicing the car, which we get done somehow without much motivation. But to achieve our full potential we must direct our energies where our heart is.

Work out when

Working out when is part of setting achievable targets, because, as I pointed out earlier, many things are possible sometime but not possible now. In fact, your success at working out when will determine to a large extent your success at the task itself. Working out when is to do with time management, priorities and planning, and it is the aspect of getting things done that many of us are worst at.

It is worth just pausing to consider why that might be. Let's imagine the objections that people might raise if asked to plan their time more effectively.

Planning and time management are for business people, not ordinary people. It's just plain silly to approach everyday life in that way.

Time is particularly important to business people, and so is getting things done. That's why they try to be systematic in their use of time, even using special time management diaries, writing computer programmes, and going on courses in their efforts to make the most of the time they have. But time is important to all of us. We all have about the same amount and we would all like to make the most of it. For each one of us, that means something different; for some, it means spending a lot of time with their children, for others, writing books, for others, reading as widely as they can, and so on. But we all want to make the most of our time – so why shouldn't we take a leaf out of the businessman's Filofax?

If I start planning out what I'm going to do it all looks too much and it puts me off even starting. I'd rather just muddle along and not look ahead.

This approach is fine, if you don't mind which things you get done and which you don't, and if you don't mind wasting time. You might be planning too far ahead, or planning too much: working out when, done right, should make things look *more* achievable, not less.

It doesn't matter how carefully I plan – something unexpected always happens and upsets the plan. Planning is a waste of time.

Working out when does not mean deciding on a rigid timetable and throwing it out of the window the minute something happens to upset it. Even major industrial projects, where time slippage costs thousands or even millions of pounds a day, are planned with some flexibility because it is recognized that unforeseen problems are bound to arise. Working out when means managing time systematic-ally but flexibly, and adjusting the plan when something unexpected happens. That kind of planning saves enormous amounts of time, in everyday life just as in the world of business and commerce.

Just one further point needs to be made before we leave the subject of why we should manage time and move onto how. Working out when is the only way to combat public enemy number one of getting things done: procrastination. If you have no plan, it's so easy to put things off again and again – and the more you put something off, the easier it is to put it off even further. If on the other hand you have undertaken to start something at a particular time, on a particular day, and maybe even rescheduled other things and organized other activities around it, you will find it much harder to let yourself down!

So hopefully you are convinced of the value of step number 4, working out when. There are an enormous number of systems for time management, many based on looseleaf diaries, some running on programmable calculators, and millions have been made by the publishers of these systems. I am sure, however, that the system which will work best will be one you develop for yourself. It will then suit. For example, if you like writing, it will involve setting out plans and times on paper, writing a note at the end of every day on progress and so on; if you don't like writing, it may be done entirely in your head and related to knots in a handkerchief (one of the earliest time management systems). You can vary your system to suit the task. Also, if you develop your own system, you will be motivated to use it, because it's yours – and, anyway, developing systems is fun so why should the authors have all the fun!

So rather than give you a system for managing your time, I shall give you twenty tips to get you started. You can build your system out of one or more of these tips, but you will probably have lots of ideas of your own you want to try.

Twenty time management tips for working out when

1. *Lists* Jot down in a list all the things you want to get done. Add to the list and cross items off as you ask yourself why, set achievable targets, and think of more things. Use the list to identify the three most important things for today, for this week, for this month, for this year. Cross things off the list as you achieve them (don't rub them out: you want to see how much you've done!)

   It doesn't matter where you write your lists: in a diary, on the back of an envelope, on a whiteboard. But don't lose them!

2. *Creating special times* Identify particular times of the day for particular things, especially for new things you haven't had time to start yet. Sometimes people find it useful to get up an hour earlier in the morning, and that 'extra' hour will be for learning a foreign language, or reading a certain book, or baking bread. Take a week off work, to finish off something. Start sending the children to Sunday school, and create a clear hour every Sunday morning. There are lots of ways to create special times – but mind you don't fall into the trap of doing ordinary things in the special times!

   Look at your typical day critically and see if there are any 'unused' bits of time. Maybe there is half-an-hour in the early morning when you just potter? You could use this time for a while to get something done. But whatever you do, don't timetable activities into every minute; we all need 'potter times', and any timetable which doesn't allow for them won't be adhered to.

3. *Manageable chunks* Break the job down into bite-sized chunks and tackle them one by one. Some people find it helpful to increase the size of the chunk day by day: 'I'll write one report today, two tomorrow, three the next day.' Others find it helpful to decrease the chunk day by day, so each day holds the promise of being easier than the day before. 'I'll paint the ceiling and two walls today, two walls tomorrow, and touch up the corners the next day.'

4. *Worst job first* Take all the things you have to do and organize them into worst first, then next worst, and so on. The thing you're looking forward to most is last. Do them in that order.

5. *Best jobs first* Sometimes it's appropriate to do it the other way round – particularly if someone might arrive later to help you!

6. *Task sandwiches* Organize your time so that you do a little bit of one job, then a bit of another, then return to the first. This style is very appropriate when there are necessary delays in jobs, such as baking, or writing and then getting your writing typed up. It's also useful with boring tasks, where you don't want to spend too much time on a single task at a stretch, and you can use one task to refresh you for the next. Here are some task sandwiches which have worked for me: writing/making phone calls/writing; weeding/pruning/weeding; washing clothes/cooking/washing clothes; working out accounts/tidying up/working out accounts. You can have double-decker or treble-decker sandwiches, of course!

Take care your sandwiches are really planned, and don't deteriorate into things never being completed.

7. *Matching tasks to time* Slot jobs or parts of jobs which will take half-an-hour into half-hour sized time slots. Wait for a whole day free before tackling something you know will take that time. Combining the 'manageable chunks' principle with 'matching tasks to time' should enable you to make the best use of the time that's there.

8. *Banishing the clock* Having a clock or watch around can

prevent you getting the job done. Banish it, and concentrate on what you're doing, not on the time it's taking. (Anything even moderately creative, such as writing letters, planning a children's party and so on, often falls into the category of tasks for which this approach is useful.)

9. *Useful clock-watching* For other tasks, you may need or want to time yourself precisely, perhaps even to pace yourself. Set yourself competitions: how fast can I mow the lawn this week? Will I get all the bills paid in the next half hour? Use alarm clocks and timers so you don't have to look at the clock continually.

10. *Pinboards, blackboards and other visual aids* Have noticeboard space round your calendar. Connect notes and reminders to the appropriate day (best day to do it/last chance to do it/whatever) with thread or a drawn line.

11. *Colourful times* Use colour, whatever your system of noting things down. Red for urgent, blue for not so urgent, yellow for things you'll enjoy doing, grey for boring tasks. Whatever categorization means most to you and is useful in planning your time, use colour to mark it out.

12. *Records* For many tasks and jobs, we don't know how long they'll take. I tend to underestimate the time I need; others allow themselves too much. Start keeping a record of how long it takes you to do things – then you can plan more effectively. Don't forget the useful distinction between elapsed time and time on task. For example, doing one load of washing may take 1.5 hours from start to finish (total or 'clapsed' time), but you only need spend a total of a quarter of an hour occupied with it (time on task or 'working time').

13. *Pictures* Pictures often clarify and motivate. Draw out the week's tasks like a ladder – each time you complete one, move a pin up a rung, or shade in the space. Plot the amount of time gone by against the amount you've achieved.

14. *Review and reschedule* There comes a time when you're so far off course you have to modify the plan. Rough guide: if the plan is annoying and confusing you rather than helping you, review it.

15. *Set targets* Ask yourself: how far do I want to have got after an hour? by the end of the morning? by the end of the week? Note it down, if it helps.

16. *Realism* The more realistic your plans are, the more useful

they will be. Never mind how much you think you ought to get done in a day; how much can you get done?

17. *Honesty* You wouldn't believe how many people cheat on their records, even though they're the only person who will see them. *Important message: cheating wastes time.* If you don't achieve what you planned to, you've learned something about your speed of working. It's nothing to be ashamed of.

18. *Varying the pace* Give yourself demanding periods, where you're asking yourself to get a lot done, and slack periods. Not only do people work better with a varied pace, but you will learn more about your preferred pace, your optimum pace, and the fastest you can manage under pressure.

19. *Pressure* Use pressure sometimes to make yourself achieve more. Ask someone to check your progress, or promise yourself an evening out if you get a certain amount done. Everybody needs a bit of pressure from time to time to achieve their best.

20. *Don't let planning replace doing* The only bad thing about planning is that it can become an end in itself – particularly if what you're planning to do is particularly difficult, crucial, or unpleasant. You will plan and replan, trying to get it just right, as a way of avoiding getting on with it. Watch out for the syndrome and when you recognize it, stop planning and start doing!

Work out how

Working out when can take some time, particularly when you're not used to managing your time. Working out how is more straight-forward, and we can describe this last step in the KR–3W five-point plan quite quickly.

Working out how is to do with practicalities. Do you have what you need (tools, equipment, materials)? This may sound trivial, but it is amazing how much failure results from overlooking simple preparation. If you're going to write letters, you need paper and envelopes; if you're going to sketch, you need pencils and drawing paper. Just pause for a few minutes before you embark on something, and visualize the activities you will engage in and what you will need. It's embarrassing to remember the number of recipes I have embarked on, only to discover, too late, that I haven't any cocoa powder, or cooking oil!

You also need to work out, before you begin, how you are going to tackle the task. If you are painting a ceiling, how will you reach? If you are researching the cost of a new car, what questions will you ask? If it seems complicated, you may find it helpful to jot down your plan of campaign, or a few minutes' reflection may well be enough. 'Look before you leap' is a sound motto here.

Importantly, as you work out how, you will be assessing whether your own particular strengths equip you well enough to get the whole job done yourself, or whether you need to enlist someone else's help. You may even decide you need to learn a new skill before you start, in which case you should return to the beginning of KR–3W to work out your plan for doing that!

Recapping

You have now, I hope, a five-point plan for getting things done, and a good understanding of why each step in the five-point plan is important. The more you employ this plan, the more it will become second nature, and it will save you time, help you to make the most of your time and give you more free time.

3

The Right Environment

The basics

There are some basic steps we can take to put ourselves into the right setting for getting things done. They may seem mundane, but if you're not achieving what you want to it could well be for just one of these mundane reasons. Imagine if Shakespeare had tried to compose sonnets while sitting on a rollercoaster (excuse the anachronism!). How crazy it would be for him to conclude that he had no talent when it was his environment that wasn't right!

So before we delve deep into the prerequisites for success, let us consider some of the simpler things in life and how they can help or hinder.

The proper name for the study of people at work is 'ergonomics', and its practitioners are known affectionately as 'ergo-gnomes'. They are responsible for such critical environments as a pilot's cockpit, the car driving seat and computer workstations. A little of their expertise will not go amiss in helping us to find the best environment for what we want to achieve.

Seating

Many of the things we may want to get done are sedentary activities – writing, reading, much talking and listening (and hence much learning), many games and so on. Ergonomists have found that good seating increases people's accuracy, endurance and motivation. A major study into the effectiveness of a multi-million pound computer system for the Royal Navy had as one of its key recommendations that seats at the consoles should be changed; the discomfort and awkwardness of the seating made the sailors tired, and could well have reduced their combat effectiveness.

So if you want to get a lot done sitting down, treat yourself to a really comfortable chair.

Lighting

Not only is adequate lighting necessary for many tasks, it cheers us up and makes us feel more like getting on with things. A dingy room is depressing and demoralizing; a bright one encourages and stimulates. Good daylight is best – a desk next to a window, or working out of doors. Failing that, arrange plenty of light – and make sure it falls on what you're looking at.

Temperature

Again, scientific research has shown that we are much less effective if we are too hot or too cold. If you are trying to be creative in an artist's garret, the muse may leave you simply because the room is too cold.

Noise

Certain kinds of noise have been shown to impair anyone's efficiency quite markedly. High-pitched noise is particularly damaging, and any sound which 'grates' or puts your teeth on edge. It is unlikely you will be able to get much done if there is a baby crying in the background, particularly if it's yours! We are 'programmed' to pay attention to that sound above most other things.

Some people are hypersensitive to noise. They really need a very quiet place, not only to ensure they get things done but to ensure they stay sane!

Putting cottonwool in your ears is only a second-best solution because you then become much more aware of the noise inside your ears and head.

Clothing

For many activities there are appropriate clothes. It pays to wear them. But whatever you are doing, make sure that what you are wearing is comfortable and allows you freedom of movement.

Work surfaces

Work surfaces at the right height, which are big enough and strong enough for what you want to do, can increase your effectiveness by 100 per cent.

Tools

It may be a 'bad workman who blames his tools' but why give

yourself unnecessary problems by using the wrong equipment or the right equipment in the wrong way? If you don't know the right way to handle a saw, an axe, a stencilling knife, a paint-roller, find out before you start or you'll waste incalculable amounts of time. Watch a young child using his knife and fork and you'll see what I mean.

Find out what suits you

Getting the basis of your environment right offers some scope to enhance your effectiveness, but adjusting it to suit your own personality and pattern of working offers far more. Some people get more done with loud music playing: it increases their general level of arousal and their ability to apply themselves. Some people like lots of fresh air – an open window is essential to them. Others like an attractive view, but that distracts yet others.

Here are some aspects of your physical environment you might like to experiment with, to see what suits you best:

- experiment with all the basics (seating, lighting, temperature, noise, clothing, work surfaces and tools), to 'fine tune' them to what suits you
- location – at home, away from home (some people make a point of going to the library, for example, to get things done without interruptions), everyday room, special room, always the same, varied (some people find it best to have a single set location for things – others find they can renew their energy and attentiveness by working in the garden in the morning, in the kitchen in the afternoon, and in the library the next day)
- level of interruption – none, some, lots
- level of visual interest around you – none, some, lots
- everything within arm's reach/reasons for walking about
- coffee- and tea-making facilities at hand/some way away/not available (yes – some people find they spend all their time making and drinking coffee if they don't banish it!)
- telephone/no phone
- able to hear front doorbell/not able
- getting everything out ready to start/having everything laid out and waiting permanently

Getting the environment right for you is an important way of controlling that persistent wanderer – your attention.

Matching the environment to the task: 'different holes for different goals'

Changing the environment in which we do something offers us a further opportunity: to match the environment to the task. Of course, we do this all the time, hence the existence of kitchens, studies and garden sheds – but I am also talking about something more subtle and more variable, aspects of the environment that we can change from day to day or task to task.

Let me give you an example. When I go to work, if I am reading, writing and studying all day, I wear trousers. Trousers make me feel more workmanlike, I focus on the job and not on my appearance – and now I have an association between trousers and study, that I can make use of. If I have a day of interviews with clients, or I am making a presentation, I wear a suit (skirt and jacket). That kind of attire makes me feel like putting on a good show, like performing in a sense.

People who change when they get home from work are using the same principle. Changing clothes can change what you are effective at. A tracksuit helps you relax; a business suit helps you assert yourself.

You can change other aspects of your physical environment to achieve the same kinds of effect. Suppose you have two letters to write. One is to the bank – the other is to your sister. Write to the bank, sitting at a table or desk in a straightbacked chair. Write to your sister curled up in an armchair by the fire.

Let us paint some pictures of some very particular environments and the kinds of achievements and activities they are right for – 'different holes for different goals!' Just one thing before we start: if you find yourself thinking as you read this section, 'Who has a house big enough to have all these places?' remember that I am describing them in their fully-fledged form. A simple change of chair can indicate a change of place, the dining room might be your 'void', the kitchen might double up as a 'hub' and 'heap' at different times of day. Sometimes, changing the environment in a very minor way, for example, taking the cloth off the kitchen table, can signal you are about to embark on a different activity and so help you get into it. The point is, you will achieve more if you use your physical environment to help you.

The den

This is a place where you and only you are allowed to go, where you leave things as you want to find them, where no one is allowed to disturb you. It may have treats in it, such as chocolates or biscuits. It is probably cosy, and likely to be in an attic or annexe. You will get your own things done there, secret projects such as present wrapping or diary-keeping, things you particularly want to achieve at for yourself. In your den, you are more likely to be effective at those things you enjoy doing than at those you find a trial.

The heap

This is a place where you can make a mess. There are no expensive furnishings to be damaged, no one will be entertained here; it is a place for doing messy things which involve bits and pieces scattered here and there, sewing, for example.

The library

Although I have called this place the 'library', it does not necessarily have books in it. But it has lots of resources relevant to what you are trying to get done, and lots of ideas and stimuli. If you are painting still life, it will have lots of different interesting objects and your own still lifes on the wall. If you are writing, it will have lots of books. If you are learning French, it will have all sorts of bits and pieces of France in it: books, maps, coins, magazines. Its function is to be like an extension of your brain.

The void

The void has nothing in it. The walls are bare, the furniture minimal. It is quiet. You can't see the street – there may even be no windows. It is for activities that require extreme sustained concentration. You might rehearse a speech here, solve a chess problem, meditate or mend a valuable ornament.

The lab

This is a place with lots of equipment relevant to your activity. It is an extension of your body. A photographic darkroom, a kitchen, a printer's studio – these are labs in the sense I mean it. Labs tend to be expensive: don't invest in one unless you are sure you want to spend lots of time using it.

The hub

This is a place in the midst of everyday life, allowing you to get things done without losing contact with those around you. It might be a favourite armchair or a kitchen table, a desk in the living room or a corner of the hall. It is essential for those activities on which you would never embark if it meant losing time with your family and friends, secondary but nonetheless important things such as knitting, crosswords and the football pools.

4

The Right Frame of Mind

Strange but true facts about the 'right' frame of mind

Supposing someone asked you what you would guess the 'right' frame of mind to be for getting things done. You might well say something along the following lines.

Well, you would need to be fairly calm – not worried about anything because that might distract you. And reasonably happy, and optimistic – pretty confident. It would help if you felt you had lots of support from people around you.

Just as a car which is well serviced and in good condition travels fastest, a healthy, strong athlete runs furthest, and a well-nourished sturdy plant grows tallest, so we might expect a well-adjusted and mature person to achieve most.

Let me tell you two true stories that challenge that view.

The angry author

Robert had worked for his present company for two years. When he joined them, he was promised promotion within twelve to eighteen months, providing he did well. He knew he had indeed done well, much better than might have been expected since his employment by this company had marked a career change for him. He had moved out of teaching into the computer industry.

Both bosses for whom he had worked since joining had given him good appraisals. The two projects on which he had worked had been successfully completed, and had resulted in further business being won for the company. He was now leading a team of three, whereas when he had started he had had no responsibility for others' work. By all normal criteria, he had done well.

Yet no promotion was forthcoming. Obviously, Robert had mentioned this to his current boss on a few occasions; each time the answer was along the lines of 'We haven't forgotten, the MD's just

36

getting round to it.' Months passed; still nothing happened.

Robert became depressed and frustrated, then angry. He felt he was being shortchanged by the company. Every month that passed was a month when he should have been on a higher salary. The more he thought about it, the more his anger increased, and he thought about it more and more.

Robert had been meaning to write a book on his hobby, fishing, for quite a few years. He had some notes at home on the outline, and the first chapter partially written. One day, when he was mulling over his unfair treatment at work, he suddenly realized what to do. He would reduce his investment in the company, since they weren't prepared to invest more in him. He would look for reward and satisfaction elsewhere. He would write his book.

No-one at work guessed that Robert had decided to do this. He continued at work full-time, continued to be competent and apparently committed. But his real energies were going into writing his book in the evenings and at weekends. He found he got most writing done just after something had happened at work to fuel his anger: for example, when he met with the MD and she didn't mention his promotion, or when he received praise from a client underlining what good work he was doing. His anger was being channelled into his book, and kept him going.

He finished the book in record time. In fact, while he was still writing it, his promotion was announced – but he held onto his anger. It was after all ten months late. It made him even more angry that now he was supposed to appear pleased and grateful.

His book was published the following year, and sold well for a book of its type. Robert often wondered if he would ever have achieved it if he had been promoted on time.

The unpopular entrepreneur

Linda had been a rather isolated, unhappy adolescent. It was difficult to put your finger on why, but she never seemed quite to fit in with the other girls at her boarding school. They weren't actively unpleasant to her; it was just that she often seemed left out of games and plans. She felt her isolation keenly and looked with some envy at more popular schoolmates.

At home too, because she was away for so much of the time, she lacked company. She had a loving family and one or two friends, but what she would have liked more than anything was to be one of a gang.

When Linda left school, she didn't go to university, although she could have done. She started a small business organizing parties and catering for special events, using some money an aunt had put in trust for her. She found demand for her services, and discovered she had quite a head for business. After a year, she took on two staff, and by the end of three years she was running an extremely successful company of twenty.

Her company had the reputation of being youthful, friendly, and informal. All the staff, including Linda, went away on holiday together at least once a year. They spent a lot of free time together, and organized lots of social events.

I think that Linda's drive to achieve and create her own business stemmed from her unhappiness at her earlier unpopularity. She was prepared to work exceptionally hard to create her own gang.

If you study the lives of successful people, people who have achieved, you find that the pattern in the two stories I have just told is the rule rather than the exception. Quite the opposite of relaxed and emotionally stable, many successful entrepreneurs are driven by a desire to escape their appalling family backgrounds or by a fundamental sense of inferiority which they have to work their whole lives to dispel. I am not talking here of people such as artists and musicians – it is well-known that exceptional creativity is often linked to instability, even madness. I am talking if you like, about ordinary high achievers, people who above everything else get lots done. And paradoxically if you were to try to work out the 'right frame of mind' from studying them, you would conclude that you needed some strong and potentially destructive emotion, such as fear or anger, to drive you to achieve.

What can we learn from these high achievers? Not, I think, that we need to find something to get angry about or that we must convince ourselves we are socially inadequate if we don't think we are already. That would be a risky course, because for every successful angry person, there are ten who waste their lives in bitterness, and for every successful person with an inferiority complex, there are ten who find a solution in violence, drink or despair. No, I think there are two lessons we can learn from all of this. I shall call them the two secrets of success.

Secret of success 1: don't wait for the perfect day

If Robert and Linda, and countless other entrepreneurs, had waited until life was just right and they felt on top of the world, they would never have started. Yet how often do we say, to ourselves or other people:

I won't start today, I'm not feeling too good.

I can't start French classes until I know we can afford our holiday.

I can't get on with my sketching while there's all this anxiety about Tim.

What we are saying in effect is, 'I'm waiting for the right time, I'm waiting for the perfect day.' Well, wait on, because there will never be one.

Don't focus on the conditions that aren't right. Make a habit of looking for the positives. You could, for example, answer each of the reasons for putting things off just quoted as follows:

If you're not feeling too good, do just a little today. Then you'll be able to say to yourself, 'Think how much more I shall achieve when I'm feeling fine.'

Learning French will mean you can start writing to a French penfriend. Then if you can't afford the holiday you planned, you can make up for it by maybe exchanging visits with your penfriend.

Use your sketching to stop your thoughts continually straying to Tim.

These kinds of comments, coming from someone else, are infuriating. They provoke in us the response, 'What do you know about it!' But if we can do this for ourselves, find reasons to get started in just about any circumstances, turn negatives to positives, and problems to opportunities, then we shall become vastly more effective.

The first secret of success lies in the 'Make the most of what is there' frame of mind.

THE RIGHT FRAME OF MIND

Secret of success 2: believe you can do it

Unless we believe we might actually achieve something, we won't get out of bed. In fact, chronically depressed people, who suffer from a conviction that nothing they can do will make anything better, take to their beds for days or weeks on end.

Of course, it is this belief that they can change things which separates the successful angry from the bitter angry, the achievers with inferiority complexes from those in despair. And who knows where this belief comes from? Maybe some people are born with it. Maybe it stems from the kinds of experiences we have when young. But it all remains a bit of a mystery, because there are those who have suffered setback after setback, and still believe; and others who have given up at the first hurdle.

Now, secret of success 2 presents us with a bit of a problem. Because if we aren't believers, how can we become so? I think it must be admitted that for those who really don't believe they can achieve, getting things done can be a long hard struggle. But fortunately most of us have, if not a firm conviction, then a reasonable hope, that we can change things. And it is this hope which we must tap, to get things done. The second secret of success lies in the 'You can do it if you try' frame of mind.

Here are some practical suggestions on how to tap it.

- Every time you achieve something, notice it. Maybe even jot it down. Notice even small things, particularly if they are new (cleaning behind the fridge, ordering something by telephone, reading a novel).
- Think of just one thing you would like to achieve. Then make sure you do it. (For many people, an adventure like climbing Everest or going on safari taps their resources of hope and belief, and they then go on to achieve more. For others, it may be something quite minor, like driving to a friend, or starting a cleaning job.)
- Think about what you have achieved in the past. Be generous to yourself! (If you make a list, don't lose it – it could come in handy when you write your CV.)
- Read biographies and autobiographies of achievers who suffered great setbacks, who turned evil into good and disaster to opportunity.

- Ask someone you trust to think of something important you have achieved in the last year.
- Imagine someone you dislike telling you that you are useless. Often anger will mobilize our resources of energy! (Remember Robert?)
- Say to yourself every morning 'Anything I want to do, I can do.' (Don't let anyone overhear – they might think you're big-headed!)
- You might find it helpful to do something with someone else. Dieters, people giving up smoking and joggers use companions in this way. Then you can 'borrow' some of their hope when yours is running low.
- Avoid seeing or hearing anything depressing for a week. Don't watch the news or read the papers. Listen to lots of cheerful, strong music. Build up some resources of optimism inside yourself.
- Look at people around you who you consider to be more successful than yourself. Allow yourself, just this once, to consider their shortcomings and disadvantages, remembering that they are getting things done in spite of these.

Some disqualifiers

Given secrets of success 1 and 2, you can turn all sorts of frames of mind to your advantage. Use the energy in anger to play your best game of tennis ever, the tranquillity of an easy mind to design a new layout for a flowerbed, the excitement of a promised love affair to carry you through the boredom of a diet.

There are some frames of mind, however, that will really get in your way. They will 'disqualify' you from the race before the starting pistol has been fired, and you will need to sort them out before you attempt to get things done.

Guilt

Guilt is a real energy-sapper. It hangs on our heart like a chain. It's particularly pernicious because, really, there's always something to feel guilty about. Parents can feel permanently guilty for not being perfect. Those of us educated according to the 'Protestant work ethic' always feel vaguely guilty when we're enjoying ourselves.

41

Anyone who has enough to eat can feel guilty about the starving millions.

I don't think I've ever heard anyone attribute even one of their achievements to guilt. It sounds peculiar somehow, 'I started up a playgroup because I felt guilty that Ben was an only child', or 'I felt so guilty I went to do voluntary work in Ethiopia.' Guilt doesn't move you forward; it sticks you firmly in the mud of the past. It saps your enjoyment of life – it is like a parrot on your shoulder squawking, 'Couldn't you do more? Couldn't you do more?'

What is there to be done, then, about guilt? If you suffer badly from it, it is worth considering professional help: a counsellor or therapist. Or you may have a friend who is close enough to you and sure enough of what is sane and sensible, who can listen to you explore your guilt and why it's there, and then help you realize how to put it to one side.

You may be able to release yourself from guilt. Some people find it helpful to draw up a sort of charter, a set of things others have a right to expect from you, and, complementarily, a set of freedoms you have a right to yourself. Here is an example of a few statements from a friend of mine's 'charter' – he found he was suffering from guilt about his younger brother, who kept asking him for help.

- My brother has a right to ask me for help.
- I have a right to refuse to give it.
- My brother has a right to talk to me when he is in trouble.
- I have a right to ask him to contact me when it is more convenient.
- My brother has a right to ask to come and stay.
- I have a right to refuse, particularly if it will upset or damage my children.

The basic idea behind charters like these, written or simply thought through, is that there are limits to what can be expected of us. It is when we measure ourselves up against standards of perfection that we are most assailed by debilitating guilt. More realistic standards enable us to be more at peace with ourselves, and to do those things we can do.

Worry

We use the word 'worry' in two senses. We speak of a dog 'worrying' an object, perhaps a rug or slipper, and of ourselves worrying about a problem, a task something we fear we cannot resolve successfully. In the first sense of the word, there is the idea of something gradually disintegrating under minor but repeated attacks. Just so does worry in the second sense cause our resolve and energy to disintegrate.

As I already remarked in Chapter 1, the best antidote to worry is action. Other secondary but possibly useful ways of overcoming worry are:

- Timetable a worry session once a day, for maybe fifteen minutes. Make yourself worry for the whole time, you may well find yourself thinking 'What on earth am I making all this fuss about?'
- Clearly think through the worst that can happen.
- Talk to someone you trust about what it is that is worrying you.
- Play with worry beads, or a worry 'egg'; it is surprising how calming little rituals like this can be.
- Impose a strict routine and stick to it; routine reassures.

Mania

This is a quite different frame of mind from guilt and worry. It is the firmly held belief that you can do anything, go anywhere, be anyone. Manic people are out of touch with reality. They can be dangerous because, at the extreme, they may try to fly or walk on water.

Most of us only know a more subdued form of mania. Sometimes it follows an outstanding success. It's very enjoyable and quite safe in moderation, but you won't achieve much when you're manic. You will only either float around on cloud nine, or take on so much in such a short time that nothing is begun, let alone finished. Enjoy it and let it pass. So long as you come back to earth reasonably soon, and your mania doesn't coincide with something you must get done, it can be a welcome break from ordinary life.

Panic

Panic is much more familiar to most of us than mania. And as we all know, you can't achieve anything when you panic. So what do you do when you feel an attack of panic coming on? You could do a lot worse than follow that age-old advice: take deep breaths, and count slowly to ten.

The key is to avoid the conditions under which panic occurs. Good time management is essential here (see Chapter 2) and, if you're the kind of person who's prone to panic, don't involve yourself in very nervewracking, demanding activities, where success or failure hinges on one word or action. You can achieve plenty in this life in calmer environments – leave the jungle to the tigers!

Daydreaming

I suffer a great deal from daydreaming. It is a very dilute form of mania, and pleasant it is too, but it does waste time.

So what can I and fellow daydreamers do about it?

- Use activity to keep your mind on the task. Don't just listen, take notes. Don't just work things out, write them down. Pace up and down; talk to yourself; it doesn't matter if the neighbours think you're mad as long as you get things done.
- Don't listen to music while you're working.
- Enjoy daydreaming when it doesn't interfere with what you want to get done – when you're gardening or painting a room, for example.

Different holes for different goals and different frames for different games

Just as in the previous chapter we saw that different physical environments, physical 'frames' if you like, suited different activities, so different frames of mind suit different activities. Gradually, as you do more, and understand what helps you and what hinders you, you will recognize what your frame of mind at any point suits you to embark on. Then you can match what you do to how you feel, and make better use of your time. Not only that, but you can begin to summon up different frames of mind when you need them. This is one of the main uses of physical frames: to encourage particular frames of mind. The 'den' will encourage calm and contentment, the 'laboratory' focused application, and so on.

The frames of mind that suit you best you will get to know, as you will get to know the physical frames that suit you. Some general points are worth making.

- High energy frames of mind, such as anger and excitement, are good for high energy tasks and anything that requires you to be creative and innovative.

- Tranquil frames of mind are necessary for sustained concentration on detail.
- Optimism is useful if you're about to try something new or difficult.
- Sad, but not depressed, frames of mind have their uses too. Write a poem; paint a picture; decide to change something. Sad frames of mind are good for reflection and thought.

5

The Right Role

Breaking the roles

If you are cast as the villain in a Victorian melodrama, you are unlikely to have much opportunity to show compassion or to do good deeds. If you are a circus clown, it seems improbable that you will be making thought-provoking political statements or developing a rich and complex character. If you are asked to play the Virgin Mary in a morality play, you won't be expecting to demonstrate your capacity for simmering lust or unbridled passion.

If the characters don't keep within their roles, the play falls apart. It is the impact of the play as a whole that matters and individuals within must accept massive constraints in the interests of making the play work.

So it is in life also: 'All the world's a stage. And all the men and women merely players.' We all have roles, many more than the single one we might have in a single play, of course, and roles that change as our lives develop (see Chapter 1, the section on 'Other people's expectations'). In any system, or team, of which we form a part, roles are necessary for the success of the enterprise: roles mean you know what to expect and don't have to spend all your time working out what's expected of you; roles make for smoother interpersonal interactions and faster communications; at their best, roles make the most of individual talents and personalities.

However, roles, by their very nature, restrict. Just as the villain in the play doesn't get to show his nice side, so the villain of the office doesn't get to show his either.

Over the last couple of decades, there has been much discussion and debate on the question of the roles of the sexes. Because each of us is either a man or a woman for the whole of his or her life, and cannot cast aside that identity, even for a moment, it is particularly important that the 'male role' and the 'female role' are not too restrictive, because any restrictions bound up with these roles will restrict us in everything we do. Generally speaking, minor roles, such as you might have on a particular committee or for a very short period of time, can be constraining without too much being lost, but major roles (husband, father, employee) need to be more flexible, more accommodating or they will stifle our creativity.

Of course, roles are not simply imposed on us. By the time we are adult, we ourselves play a major part in determining not only which role we shall have but also which roles are available. As children we fill the spaces which have been created for us by others: middle child, sensible one, rebel. But then we seek either to re-enact or escape (often by taking an opposite role) the roles we had as children. We do this in the context of the systems we come to be part of as adults. Maybe the office didn't have a rebel until we came along; in we blast, and suddenly it does, and everyone else's role adjusts accordingly. Now there's a rebel, someone has to be an authority figure. One will soon be created.

You can see how complex and subtle the 'casting process' is in real life. It is the result of many, many little interactions between the individuals in a system. Each one of us has *some* responsibility for and influence over the roles we adopt, and it is worth exploring how we can use that responsibility and influence positively.

A great deal has been written about roles and their implications for healthy, fulfilled, sane living. I want to consider them here from the point of view of getting things done. This chapter is called 'The right role' because you have to make sure you are playing the right role for what you want to achieve. If your role is the helpless, appealing blonde, mastering motorcycle maintenance will be extremely difficult for you. If your role is the hail-fellow-well-met-life-and-soul-of-the-party, you may struggle to pass a philosophy A level. To get things done, you may need to break a role or two.

Recognizing roles

The first step in ensuring you are not restricted in a way you don't want to be by your role is recognizing the roles you have, in the systems where you spend most of your time. By system, I mean group of people with some stability, some continuity in your life. Family of origin and family of creation are two obvious ones (and the role restrictions entailed by being the 'middle child' and the 'baby of the family' are well documented); other important systems are likely to be your work organization and your social group. Depending on how separate different groups within these systems are, you may have different roles within these different groups. For example, you might have one role at the tennis club, another at the bridge club, or one role in the everyday office and another role when seconded to an organizational task-force.

So, if there's something you want to achieve, something you wish you could do but can't, first identify which system you're 'in' when you're trying to achieve it. Location is often the key here – if you're at home, you're probably 'in' your family, at work, 'in' the work system. Alternatively the people who take most interest in how you try to do it will determine which system it is (whatever the location happens to be).

Having identified the system, you want to identify your role. Here are some ways to do this.

Look out for labels

If you have an affectionate label, this is a very good indicator of your role. It may be a rather unoriginal one, such as 'brick' or 'wimp' or 'dozy'; it may be something new, if the system you are in comprises a lot of creative people. I knew one social group where each person had a bird's name for a nickname, and I vividly remember how anxious one of them became when he began to realize the full significance of being the 'buzzard'. Even if you don't have a full-blown nickname or label, have a good think about the adjectives that are most often applied to you. Even positive adjectives can indicate a restrictive role – a very good friend of mine is often referred to as 'unselfish', 'giving', 'loving' and even 'saintly'. I sometimes wonder at what point she has the right to take from others.

Take a direct approach

If the system you are thinking about is fairly open and honest, you can take a direct approach and ask other people in it what role they think you have. However, when faced with a direct question like this, people will often deny the existence of roles: 'What do you mean? You're just, well, you.' You might get further by discussing the differences and similarities between individuals in the group more generally, and keep an eye out for adjectives again.

Play with images

Imagine everyone in the system were an animal. Which animal would you be? Imagine you all constituted a building. What kind of building and which part of it are you? Foundation stone, window, door, wall? What about a garden? Are you the lawn, a thornbush, a weed? If you can persuade other people to play this game with you, it is even more illuminating, but be careful. It can yield some powerful insights and they might be painful.

Look for patterns

Are there things you always do, at work for example? Are you always the one to make the first cup of coffee? Are you the one who reminds people of meetings and appointments? Are there things you never do? Are you ever first to leave the office? Ever last? Do you always argue against proposals, never for them?

Test out your theory

If you think you've identified some aspect of your role but you're not sure, try changing and see what reaction you get. If you're right you'll almost certainly provoke comments. Other people may be surprised, annoyed, angry or even especially pleased.

A dead giveaway

When you find yourself saying something like, 'Oh, don't ask me. Pete's the one who does that sort of thing . . .', then you know something very definite about your role there!

Working out whether there's a problem

Suppose you want to earn some money. You haven't been working for the last few years, but the children are all at school now and you want to go back to work part-time. But you somehow can't get it organized: you're not sure what to apply for, you don't quite ever get round to writing a letter of application or a CV, the weeks are slipping by and you aren't making any progress. So you certainly have a problem.

But does it have anything to do with your role? Let's suppose, again, that you have identified your role in the family. You are the domestic problem solver and facilitator. You sort everything out for your husband and children so they can go off to work and school and achieve. You make sure meals are ready at the right time, clothes are clean, you keep a record of appointments, clubs, commitments, and remind them all, you look after them when they are ill.

Now ask yourself – would having a part-time job conflict with that role? If the answer is 'yes', you have two choices: modify the role or give up the idea of a part-time job.

This is a rather obvious example, but in fact it is quite a common type of 'role conflict'. But the key question always when you're working out whether you have the 'right role' to get a particular thing done is, 'Is there conflict between what I want to do and my present role?'

As you probably would guess, I'm in favour of modifying roles rather than giving up on possibilities. However, before I suggest ways to break out of a restrictive role, I would just say that it is perfectly reasonable to make sacrifices for particular roles which are very important to us. We just need to be sure we want to make those sacrifices.

Breaking out

If you've decided the role you occupy in the relevant system is stopping you getting something important done, there is a range of ways you can respond, from slightly modifying your role to leaving the system.

Use a natural break

You can wait for an opportunity to occur naturally to revise your role. A new person joining the system or someone leaving present opportunities – you can use the change to alter the way you fit in. If you're the 'faithful lieutenant', for example, and the 'general' leaves, you might step into the general's shoes, or at least step out of those of the lieutenant. A businessman I know had never chaired a meeting, because it was well known amongst his colleagues that he had a debilitating stammer. Then one day a new boss arrived, who knew nothing about the stammer, and he asked the businessman to chair the first progress meeting. The stammer caused no particular difficulty, and the businessman turned out to be rather a good chairman. But as long as his primary role had been as 'the stammerer', he had never considered putting himself forward.

Natural breaks also occur when circumstances change. Crises, threats, holidays – all these shake up the system, and if you're quick off the mark they allow you to change roles.

Negotiate

You may choose to negotiate a change of role openly with others in the system. Housewives returning to work often do this with their families, employees with their bosses. It will only work if people around you are prepared to acknowledge that roles can be restrictive, and that they're not part of some 'natural order'. You will need to negotiate for others to change their roles too – after all, if you stop being the 'forward thinker' for everyone else, they will have to start doing a bit of forward thinking for themselves.

Avoid the system

Suppose you are the 'baby of the family' but you want to learn mountain climbing, where taking responsibility and showing initiative are the essence. You might not want to put lots of effort into stopping being the baby of the family just so that you can be a successful climber. So you can 'avoid' your family role by engaging in mountain climbing as a completely separate activity. Don't tell your family much about it, and don't invite them to watch you. Avoid the system which holds you back.

Keep systems separate

This is an extension of the previous point. You are likely to be capable of a much wider variety of achievements if you have several quite distinct roles. You may achieve advantageous deals in tough negotiations at work; at home, you may achieve woodwork and painting. You may be the chairman of the golf club, but just one of the crowd at the drama club. Don't let your role in one system 'infect' all the other systems, or you will never find out the depth and breadth of your potential. If you're always a 'mother figure' or always the 'leader', you are limiting yourself and limiting what you can achieve. One of the biggest problems for people in public life is that a single role, the one seen by everyone, takes over their whole life and robs them of the chance to try out other roles.

Find someone to take over your role

One of the most effective ways of curing a phobia is to find someone who is even more phobic than you are. I was terrified of spiders until I went on holiday with a young girl who was even more terrified of them. Seeing her shriek and rush out of the room made me feel positively calm, and I scooped spiders of all sizes up in glass jars, transferred them to the garden and reassured my travelling companion. Since that experience, I have been much less frightened of spiders generally.

My travelling companion had taken over my role of 'person needing saving'. You can use this effect to your advantage. Suppose you wish you could become more organized. Find someone, or a group of people, who are less organized than you are. Arrange to undertake something jointly with them. You will be amazed at how quickly you change!

We often tend to attach ourselves to groups or individuals who complement our own characteristics. A very creative manager will accumulate a set of good administrators around her. An impractical man will marry a very practically minded wife. In order to develop in our areas of relative weakness, we need to reverse this pattern, and seek out people who are like us, only more so – not the whole time, of course, but some of the time.

Abandon the system

This is an extreme remedy for breaking the restrictive role. But it is often used. People leave marriages, leave home, leave their jobs, frequently to escape the constraints an apparently immutable role has forced upon them. If you've tried everything else and failed, you may have to abandon the system; But beware, very often people leave one system only to join another one exactly the same.

It is worth remembering if you are in a group that has been abandoned that you now have a chance to achieve all kinds of things which were formerly the province of the person who has left (see also above, 'Use a natural break'). Sometimes divorce turns out to be a real boost to the personal effectiveness of the person left behind, for that very reason.

A dictionary of roles

As a further aid to recognizing roles and understanding the ways different roles will set constraints on what you can achieve, I have compiled a brief 'role dictionary' of examples. You may recognize one of your roles here, or the examples may lead you to work out your own unique roles. (Role-spotting is quite a fun pastime – next time you're watching a group of people, see if you can guess each one's role in that group!)

Baby: indulged but never taken seriously, you won't get much done at all in this role. You'll get your own way, but it won't feel like much of an achievement.

Boss: (top-dog, leader) you may be paid to be the boss in certain contexts, you may choose to be in others. But don't get trapped in this role: you won't be able to achieve much yourself because you'll be expected to be giving orders. This can be a surprisingly restrictive role.

Brainbox: you're the one with the good ideas, the one who reads, writes and researches things. You know answers to factual questions, and your arguments are renowned for their logic. In this role you'll find it difficult to achieve anything 'irrational', and your spontaneity may be stifled.

Clown: good fun to be this in some groups, but like the baby you won't be taken seriously. You won't be allowed to direct the project or take responsibility for seeing something through.

Delinquent: you're good at breaking things: plans, projects, consensus. You won't be able to build in this role.

Devil's advocate: people turn to you to test out their ideas and plans but you have a reactive not a creative role, and you are on the sidelines of group activity.

Dogsbody: (doormat, gofer, sucker) you may get a great deal done, but none of it because you *want* to do it.

Godfather: you may be asked to find things, provide accommodation or backing for other people's projects. You won't be able to get your hands dirty or know the satisfaction of doing something yourself.

Martyr: unmatchable in your ability to get things done for others, you will find it impossible to do something just for you. This role is a real trap, because it keeps you very busy and makes you feel needed – but at tremendous cost to your own potential to achieve.

Mr/Miss Awkward: you're different from devil's advocate in that you're not much use. This is an easy role to get into, but you need to get out of it fast because it will prevent you achieving anything constructive.

Odd one out: you are the eccentric, the one who's different, who breaks the group's rules. You will be good at achieving things on your own but find it difficult in a group or team, so quite a lot of doors will be closed to you from the point of view of getting things done.

Old faithful: this role means you will achieve a lot in a steady reliable way, but you are unlikely to surprise, innovate, do anything daring, dangerous, or adventurous. Don't be misled by the nickname: young people can be old faithfuls too.

Passenger: you just hitch a ride on other people's ideas, enthusiasms and hard work. You are totally ineffective in this role.

Plodder: you get things done, but slowly. If you find people around expect you to be slow, make a real effort to break out by finding something you're quick at, or work all through the night and surprise them.

Practical organizer: you're a very useful person to the group, but you will find it hard to be irresponsible. You also may be kept so busy that there's no space left for being creative.

Shadow: you boost the group's numbers but that's about all you do. If you find you're a shadow in a lot of groups, you may need to go on an assertiveness training course, or find a group of people even more quiet and retiring than yourself.

Star: what a wonderful role to have! But wait – it may mean you have fans rather than friends, and it may prevent you achieving something rewarding but unostentatious like reorganizing the filing system or editing someone else's work. Don't be a star in every system.

Team player: you are the opposite of the odd one out. You are good at achieving things in the group, but bad at achieving things independently.

Weakling: lots of groups need someone to look after, and you are it. Whilst you occupy this role, you won't be allowed to achieve anything that requires strength or stamina.

Whizzkid: you tend to specialize in spectacular one-offs rather than sustained moderate achievement. You're not very good at keeping your house clean but you cleared out a friend's shed in record time. You introduced a stunningly good financial software package at work but you still haven't produced the user documentation.

Remember: by a 'role' is meant a set of expectations others have about you and you have about yourself in a particular social context. Don't mistake a role for a permanent feature of personality: one of the major achievements of psychologists has been to show conclusively that people behave very differently in different settings. A low achiever at school may be a high achiever in the football team, a 'passenger' at the office may be the 'leader' of the sailing club. Of couse, we are all of us naturally predisposed to take on certain roles rather than others, but that's exactly why we must force ourselves to break out to explore our full potential.

6
Keeping Going

Getting started is one thing; what often lets us down is our inability to keep going until we have finished. Persistence, tenacity, commitment, call it what you will: it's a vital key to getting things done. And as is the case with many 'keys to success', there are no infallible tricks, no magic wands. What this chapter does is bring together a whole collection of ideas and suggestions, things which have worked for me and for others sometimes (but not every time), pitfalls and ways out of them that have been experienced by some people who have succeeded at keeping going sometimes (but not every time), and practical tips that will sometimes (but not every time) give you that little nudge you needed when you were about to come to a standstill. Look on this chapter as two things. First, as a comforter (feeling like giving up is one of the worst things in the world; this chapter can help you work out why you're feeling that way, and reassure you that other people have been there too). Second, as a toolkit (your will to succeed has broken down; somewhere in here you may well find the spanner, screwdriver, or hammer to mend it).

Have you got a problem keeping going? Or are you one of those rare individuals who finishes everything she starts? Answer this quick quiz and find out.

Tenacity quiz

1. When was the last time you gave up on a project (any project, for example: reading a book, learning a new skill, cleaning a room before breakfast every day), leaving it unfinished?

   (a) Less than a week ago
   (b) More than a week but less than a month ago
   (c) More than a month ago

2. How many unfinished projects have you got on at the moment?

   (a) More than ten
   (b) More than two
   (c) Two or fewer

3. Do you feel disappointed about things you have started but given up on?

   (a) All the time
   (b) Often
   (c) Occasionally

4. Do other people expect you to complete what you undertake?

   (a) Never
   (b) Occasionally
   (c) Most of the time

5. How many projects have you successfully completed this year?

   (a) None
   (b) One
   (c) More than one

6. Which of the following adjectives describes your pattern of working best?

   (a) Lazy
   (b) Variable
   (c) Disciplined

If you answered mostly (a)s or (b)s, then you have a problem keeping going. If you answered mostly (c)s, either you don't start much in the first place (in which case, reread the first five chapters of this book!) or you already know how to see things through (in which case, skip to Chapter 7).

It's easy to assume that when we give up on something, or shelve it indefinitely, the problem lies with us, that we somehow just don't have what it takes to keep going. This is a counsel of despair, and I reject it. In fact, there are all sorts of good reasons why projects are abandoned, and we can do plenty to reduce the number of things we fail to get done. Let's look at some of these good reasons, and then pull together a set of guidelines to make sure that we can keep going when we want to.

Reasons for not getting things done

Lack of conviction

Lack of conviction accounts for many of the unfinished novels in bottom drawers, plans for gardens and extensions filed behind the telephone, and application forms for new jobs lying on desks, gathering dust. When we start a new project, our own enthusiasm is often enough to get us going, and the novelty value is also working in our favour. As we get into the job, we become conscious of the time and effort we're investing in it, and we begin to ask ourselves, 'Is there really any point? Aren't I just wasting my time?' We want the prospect of a real return on our investment if we're going to go on, and if we aren't convinced there is one, we give up.

When we come to this point we need to take time out of the task in hand to establish the likelihood of success. If you're writing a novel, contact some agents and discuss possibilities with them. Talk to friends who've written books and had them published. If you're planning an extension, investigate the finances. How much will it cost? How likely is it you will get a loan? Do some basic research so that you're in a better position to know if your investment will pay off. If you still lack conviction after you've done this, you may be better off consigning that novel to the bottom drawer, or abandoning the extension.

It's taking much longer than you thought

Lots of jobs and projects invite us to underestimate the time we need to complete them. Tidying and sorting jobs fall into this category par excellence, because once we start them we unearth all sorts of hidden messes and muddles that need to be dealt with. Other projects that typically 'grow' unpredictably are learning projects (can you realistically estimate how long it will take you to learn a new language to fluency, or learn to play the piano?) and 'mystery' projects where you embark on something without really knowing what it entails (joining committees can be like this!).

Obviously we need to try and be as realistic as possible when estimating how long something will take to get done. It's a good idea to keep a record of how long things typically take you, if you're often getting it wrong (see 'Work out when' in Chapter 2). But this won't help you for totally new projects. So what do you do when you find the job's taking much longer?

Sometimes you can speed up the pace at which you work. Sometimes you can choose to accept a lower standard in the interests of finishing. Or you may redefine the 'finishing point' – perhaps not fluency but ability to understand others, perhaps not the whole cupboard, just the top two drawers.

It's a pity if you have to give up altogether because it's taking too long. After all, you will then have lost all the time you've put in so far. If a project turns out to be much bigger than you had first foreseen, maybe it is in fact more worthwhile, more important than you realized. Thinking about that may give you the extra boost of motivation you need to see it through.

Enthusiasm leads to disenchantment

Have you ever bought all the materials you need to start, for example, painting in oils, attempted one or two paintings in a rather desultory fashion, and then consigned the materials to a box, never to be reopened? Sometimes the extremity of our initial enthusiasm, and even the expensiveness of the equipment we have bought, seem to result directly in subsequent disenchantment. It's as if we were expecting too much from the activity.

There is also a related, particularly damaging pattern we can sometimes find ourselves caught up in. I call it the 'buying instead of doing' pattern. We want change, we want to have an effect on what's around us, and we want it all to happen quickly, so we rush off and buy things that appear to promise change and achievement. We buy a new electric drill, a saw, a sander, when maybe we should just be putting up that old shelf in the garage with the tools we already have. We buy a cookery book instead of baking some biscuits. There are two problems with this pattern: it's expensive, and it doesn't actually lead us toward achieving anything. In fact, it leads us away, as we become more and more committed to buying instead of doing.

If you think you've fallen into this pattern, make sure the next project you embark on doesn't require any capital expenditure at all. You'll probably finish this one.

The law of diminishing returns

There are some kinds of jobs where the early stages are very rewarding, but as the job progresses the rewards seem to decline. Painting a room can be like this. The first coat of paint works an amazing transformation, the second coat less of one, and the third, which is needed for a truly professional effect, doesn't seem to make much difference at all. When you're attempting to master a new skill, peaks and troughs of progress are very common, and during a trough you're very likely to give up altogether.

This is where what I call 'manufactured' rewards come in very handy. There are two kinds of reward to most activities. The first kind is bound up with the nature of the task itself, it is intrinsic to the task. Learning how to drive means that you can drive a car, you can get about independently, and you have the sense of achievement associated with it. Painting the house means you have a nice attractive clean-looking house. Walking the dog means the dog has had good exercise. These are all examples of intrinsic or 'natural' rewards. 'Manufactured' rewards are rewards that you, or someone else, has associated artificially with the task. After each driving lesson, you treat yourself to a glass of wine. After each wall is painted, you put your feet up for an hour with a book. When you've walked the dog, you make yourself a cup of coffee.

We often expect ourselves to work away without manufactured rewards. We make sure our children have them, maybe even make sure they are there for friends, family and colleagues, but somehow it doesn't seem appropriate to organize them for ourselves. It's childish, or self-indulgent.

Well, in fact, it's often just plain necessary if any jobs are going to be completed. And there's nothing wrong with manufactured rewards – if we don't use them, we're robbing ourselves of one of the most effective and flexible motivators. The problem with intrinsic rewards is that their timing is inflexible. You won't be able to drive a car alone until after you've passed your driving test. You won't be able to play a piano concerto unless you've done hundreds of hours of practice. Conversely, most of the intrinsic reward in decorating a room happens early in the process. So arrange little manufactured treats to overcome those troughs and those diminishing returns. I motivated myself to put a third coat of paint on the bedroom walls by telling myself I couldn't do any decorative stencilling on them until the three coats were finished. A year later, I still haven't done any stencilling, but the manufactured 'carrot' worked nonetheless! The walls have three coats of paint.

Boredom

Let's face it, some jobs are just plain boring. You want to do them because you want the end result, but you're overcome by boredom halfway through. Knitting, weeding, proofreading – everyone's got their own list of ten most boring tasks.

If you don't need to concentrate totally then combine boring jobs with something more interesting: do your weeding in pairs, first your garden then mine, so you can talk while weeding; listen to the radio or play music while you're knitting. Imagine how boring driving must have been before the car radio – now it's one of the best opportunities for an hour or two of totally undisturbed listening.

If you need to concentrate on a boring activity, you can't risk doing something else simultaneously. You will have to work out how long you can stand it for at a stretch, and then schedule breaks as manufactured rewards. In the breaks try to do something totally different: if you're proofreading, do aerobics in the breaks!

You didn't want to do it in the first place

It's easy to convince ourselves we want to do something before we start. It may take only a little pressure from the boss, from our friends, and we commit ourselves, even make a start. But as the task unfolds we realize that we don't really want to do it at all – and it's but a short step from there to giving up.

It may well be the only course of action. But next time, make sure you stick to KR–3W – especially 'work out why'! (see Chapter 2)

You've taken on too much

There are particular times and situations when we are especially likely to take on too much. New beginnings are such times. When you start a new job, your desk is clear, your in-tray empty. You are eager to please, and you take on anything that comes your way. A few weeks downstream, when you have your fair share of phone calls, enquiries and general admin, you suddenly realize you're overloaded. You're never going to get everything done that you took on at the start. Not only that, but you've acquired yourself the reputation in the office of being 'willing'. People keep asking you to do little extras.

Similarly, any situation where you are particularly keen to please or make a good impression can lead you into this trap. Perhaps you've just finished a set of major exams, and you want to show your family you've got time for them. You offer to cook dinner twice a week, play football with the boys, dig a new vegetable patch, reorganize the hi-fi. It's too much, and one by one your good resolutions are broken.

It's easy to say 'Don't take on too much' but of course it is part of 'working out when' to limit what you undertake to do. But what do you do when you find yourself overloaded? You do one or more of five things.

- Give some things up, but not all (later in this chapter we will talk about constructive giving up).
- Alter the timescales and deadlines.
- Do less of everything you've undertaken to do.
- Involve some more people, divide and delegate.
- Go to bed later or get up earlier.

But remember Chapter 4 and don't panic. Everyone with any kind of wish to achieve takes on too much from time to time.

Setbacks

It is hard to think of any enterprise of significance which hasn't been subjected to at least one major setback. However, the problem is that other people's achievements look like 'plain sailing' from the outside. But you only have to listen to a successful person talking about how they became successful to realize that setbacks are the very stuff of achievement. Yet they throw us, dishearten us, make us want to give up.

What can we do when we suffer the setbacks?

Think our way over them. Tell yourself that the setback is itself a sign you are making progress. In many situations, this is indeed true. Mountains get steeper towards the top.

Talk our way over them. Often what you need most when you suffer a setback is a simple encouraging comment from a good friend. 'Of course you'll succeed. It's just a temporary hitch, it happens to everyone.'

Work our way through them. Work twice as hard, just briefly, just to get beyond the hump.

Mood swing

Like setbacks, swings of mood are fairly inevitable. On some days you feel confident and full of energy, on others you feel lethargic and depressed. Our swings of mood are caused by many things: diet, the weather, events, mild infections, time of day. Depending on how extreme they are, you can either give in to them or fight them. The one assurance you need to hang on to is that your mood will always swing back again. If, in your black moods, you find yourself doubting whether you will ever achieve anything again, start to keep a 'mood diary'. If you can begin to predict your moods, not only will you have evidence that no mood lasts forever, but you may be able to begin to exert some influence over them. Never waste a good day! Those energetic, confident moods won't last forever either.

Change of circumstances

I know a father who embarked on building a climbing frame for his children. It took him some time, because he wasn't very skilled at do-it-yourself. When he was halfway through a new children's playground was set up in the village where he and his family lived. There were a wonderful climbing frame, swings, slide and mini adventure playground.

Here then is a classic example of a change of circumstances which removes the reason you had for starting a project in the first place. Only you can judge, for any individual case, whether you should give up on what you had started, or carry on maybe for a different reason from the original one. The father in my story completed the climbing frame and gave it to a local children's home.

Too few rewards, too little stimulation

Some projects, while they don't appear boring to start with, turn out to offer surprisingly little in the way of rewards or stimulation. Many essentially solitary pursuits, like dieting or doing exercises, suffer from this shortcoming.

You could use artificial rewards as was suggested in the section on 'diminishing returns' (p.59 ff.). Alternatively, you could team up with someone else, so at least there are social rewards and stimulation. Weightwatchers' clubs are based on this principle.

Another tactic that dieters often adopt, and which can usefully be borrowed for other pursuits on which it's difficult to keep going, is to keep detailed and meticulous records of progress. Dieters will chart every last calorie they consume, and draw graphs of their weight loss daily. Authors might reward themselves with a word count every few hours, joggers with records of time and distance jogged each day. Recordkeeping can introduce a new dimension of interest and reward to the most unlikely of jobs: I once knew a home cook who kept details of everything she had ever baked when she baked it, and how 'successful' or not it was. (By the way, if you want to save but find money just slips through your fingers, start keeping records of every penny you spend. It works wonders!)

Tips on keeping going

Everything you undertake, and every stage of everything you undertake, tests your ability to keep going and lays different obstacles in your path. Next time you're tempted to give up on something or you're finding the going tough, cast your eye down this checklist of tips, mottoes and reminders: you may find something there to keep you on track.

- Take time out to investigate the likelihood of success, and what success will mean.
- Speed up (and get it over with).
- Slow down (you may be trying to get things done too quickly).
- Do less.
- Don't aim for perfection.
- 'Setbacks are a sign of progress.'
- Lower your expectations.
- Build in some rewards along the way.
- Think of a really severe punishment if you don't keep going! (no television for a week, no sweet things, no evenings out for a month). (Of course, you may simply neglect to administer the punishment, in which case this approach won't work. But it does work for some people, and in an interesting way. Often we get ourselves into a vicious circle, where we give up, feel miserable about giving up, and become even less able to achieve anything because of loss of self-esteem. Sometimes by punishing ourselves

we can break that cycle. The punishment closes the book on that single episode of failure, and enables us to start afresh. Give it a try: it might work for you, it might not.)

- Find a partner.
- Break the monotony with bursts of something else.
- 'Chunk' the job differently (for example, spend only half-an-hour on it at a time, rather than an hour, or spend a whole day, really making progress).
- Find a boss or a bully (more on this shortly).
- Find a friend to jolly you along.
- Record progress, every millimetre of it.
- Draw up a detailed plan that will take you through to completion.
- Think of some more reasons why you should go for it. 'The reasonable man adapts himself to the world: the unreasonable one persists in trying to adapt the world to himself. Therefore, all progress depends on the unreasonable man' (George Bernard Shaw). So grit your teeth and prepare to be unreasonably persistent!
- 'You can never disappoint anyone so much as yourself.'
- Write down everything you've done on the job so far.
- Don't aim for completion, aim for the next stage.

Using other people's expectations

In Chapter 5, we talked about breaking out of roles that restrict us. There is a positive side to roles, which we can use to great advantage to ensure we keep going.

Imagine you had told all your friends and colleagues you were going to play the piano. You keep them informed of your progress and of how keen you are. You tell them it's your ambition to play well enough to entertain yourself and your family. You talk about how relaxing and fulfilling playing an instrument is. In fact, you become notorious as a bit of a 'piano bore'.

Now imagine you want to give it up. You've had six months of lessons, and you find you just can't practise enough. Somehow you don't feel like it, and it's not going as well as you had hoped.

How *can* you give it up? You will be a laughing stock. So other people's expectations may keep you going when your own motivation fails you.

People who are trying to give up smoking often make use of the enormous social pressures others can exert. You can use the expectations of others to support any endeavour – and even if you didn't tell anyone at the beginning, if you feel your resolve weakening, tell at least one person whose opinion is important to you what you intend to achieve. Don't tell him you'd like to achieve it, or hope to achieve it – that would leave you an escape route. Hem yourself in with his expectations.

This is what I mean by 'Find a boss or a bully'. Better still, find a whole system that will support you, and prevent you giving up. We saw the *destructive* power of social systems in Chapter 5; now you can harness their *constructive* power.

Giving up

It may seem strange to end a chapter on 'keeping going' with a section on 'giving up'. But sometimes giving up is the most sensible course of action, if you've really lost heart, if circumstances have fundamentally changed, or if there's something more important you want to do instead. If you never allow yourself to give up, then you can never allow yourself to make mistakes, and that probably means you can't allow yourself to learn.

But if you're going to give up, you must do it positively. This is important for your self-esteem and confidence, and hence your ability to undertake and achieve other things; it is also important because you do not want other people to think of you as 'someone who gives up'.

What do I mean by giving up positively? I mean making a definite decision to give up and announcing it, rather than just letting things slide. And always give a reason for giving up, if possible linking it with something else you will definitely achieve. You might, for example, say, 'I'm not going to revise for my geography exam, because it's much more important for me to do well in history.' Or you might say, 'I've decided I need to spend more time with my family. I'm going to stop attending those evening industrial society meetings.'

I remember a time when a particularly unsympathetic boss accused me of being a 'black hole'. He meant that I took on a large number of tasks, which then disappeared without trace with no evidence of any achievement. Had I been clear about what I was giving up and why, I don't think I would have been referred to as a 'black hole'.

PART TWO

How to Get Other People to Do Things

7

Why it Matters to Be Able to Get Other People to Do Things

Introduction: links with Chapters 1 to 6

Much of what has been said in the first six chapters of this book, on the KR–3W plan, on motivation and persistence, on time management and personal effectiveness, can be turned around to apply to getting other people to do things. Hopefully, having read Chapters 1 to 6, you will already be seeing other people as well as yourself in a new light, appreciating how much potential they have, and how it can be realized.

The next four chapters look at some issues specific to getting other people to do things. The information they contain, combined with everything in Chapters 1 to 6, should make you a force to be reckoned with!

The effectiveness web

Imagine a spider sitting at the centre of her web. If she could only catch flies which came within an arm's (leg's?) reach, she would soon starve. But she has increased her effectiveness as a flycatcher enormously, by extending her influence out in the form of a web. The larger the web, the more flies she will catch. So it is with getting other people to do things. If we confine what we achieve to things we can achieve by our own physical efforts, we probably won't even survive. So we need to extend our influence out, through involving other people. The wider our web of contacts and the more effectively we can get them to do things, the more we shall achieve what is important to us in life.

Try drawing your own effectiveness web. (See example on p. 72).

The more frequently you try to get someone or some group of people to do things, the closer you should put them to you in your web. It may be more meaningful to you if you put in individuals'

71

An effectiveness web

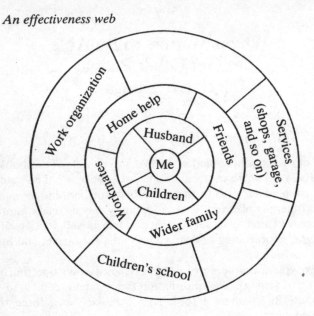

names rather than job titles or group names. You may notice a number of things about your web.

First, the people 'closest' to you may well not be the people you are confident of being able to get to do things. You may find it virtually impossible to get your husband to do anything you want him to, while it is fairly easy for you to get the garage to do what you want. We shall be looking later on in this chapter at why it is sometimes difficult to influence, persuade, advise or get help from the very people on whom we are most dependent. In the following chapters, we shall discuss how it can be made easier.

Second, you may be surprised either at how large or how small your web is. There are great individual differences in how widely people spread their influence, in this sense. Some people are quite isolated and negotiate with the rest of the world through just one or two close members of the family or friends. Others spread their web far, have fingers in many pies and form the hub of a great spinning wheel of activity. A cousin of mine provides employment for nearly everyone in the small village in which she lives, organizes holidays and projects for a wide circle of friends and is a governor of the local school. She is a truly effective spider! On the whole, a larger web is better, because you have more chance of getting the right person for any particular job and you are less likely to overload one or two individuals. If your web is very small, it may be because you aren't at all comfortable with getting other people to do things. Perhaps it embarrasses you or makes you feel guilty, perhaps you believe you can do everything better yourself. Hopefully the chapters that follow will change attitudes like these.

Third, you may have found it difficult to draw a web at all. Some people see themselves only as doing what others tell or ask them to, never reversing the process and getting anyone else to do what they determine. Whether this is true, or just the way you see yourself, again, hopefully, the remaining chapters will show you how to become, and feel, much less of a dogsbody.

When you have drawn a general effectiveness web, draw one out for yesterday. Try to remember everyone you tried to get to do something, and mark them on the web. If there were people you tried to get to do several things, put them nearer the centre.

If you find drawing these webs illuminating, draw them for different situations: a typical week at work, a family holiday, a weekend. The patterns can surprise you. A colleague of mine realized, after drawing up a work-effectiveness web, that he always asked the same person in his project team to do things, even though there were four of them, all equal members. He had to make a conscious effort to spread his demands more evenly.

Common pitfalls in getting other people to do things

Although it is such a universal and necessary activity, getting other people to do things is fraught with problems. And the problems can have extremely serious consequences, ranging from an argument to a divorce, from a wasted morning to a lost fortune!

Let us look at some of the common pitfalls, to impress upon ourselves that there's an art to getting people to do things.

Genuine misunderstanding

It is surprisingly difficult for two people to arrive at a common understanding of a task. We have all played the party game, 'Grandmother's whispers'. Something rather like it happens whenever we try to get anyone to do anything. A typical conversation would go like this.

Person A: Could you clean the windows for me?
Person B: Yes, sure.
          (Some time later.)
Person A: I thought you said you'd clean the windows?
Person B: Yes, I have.
Person A: But this one hasn't been touched!
Person B: Oh sorry – did you mean those windows? I thought you just meant the kitchen windows.
Person A: I meant *all* the windows. Why on earth did you think I meant just the ones in the kitchen?
Person B: (defensive) I don't know.

In fact, what person B has forgotten is that they were standing in the kitchen when the original conversation took place and person A waved her arms in the direction of the kitchen windows. But the damage is now done. Person A feels annoyed and let down, person B annoyed and guilty.

In Chapter 8 we shall be looking at ways to avoid misunderstandings.

Not-so-genuine misunderstanding

Now we all know the irritation and even rage produced in us by the person who deliberately misunderstands what we ask him to do. Of course, it is some people's way of avoiding work, and for others it represents rebellion, a fundamental refusal to be controlled or directed by anyone else.

Please go to bed,
Oh – did you mean right now?
Yes!
(half-an-hour later)
Are you in bed?
Yeah.
(fifteen minutes later)

But you haven't taken your clothes off!
You never asked me to.

This is an obvious example, and it is pretty clear who's being unreasonable in this exchange. In fact, it sounds like an exchange between an adult and a child, which is hardly surprising since misunderstanding on purpose is an essentially 'childish' habit which children develop as a natural extension to earlier genuine misunderstanding. However, this does not stop adults from doing it. Indeed not-so-genuine misunderstanders can be very subtle, and it is often difficult to distinguish them from the genuinely confused. Chapter 8 looks at how to deal with them.

One-way traffic

It is easy to fall into a pattern with family, friends and neighbours where help and support only travel in one direction. This is very destructive of equal relationships. If you are always getting your husband to do things, but he never gets you to do anything, then you are in charge. Do you want to be in charge in your marriage, or would you rather share responsibilities equally? If a friend of yours is always asking you to babysit, walk the dog, feed the fish, but you ask nothing of her, the 'friendship' is likely to deteriorate.

Some people avoid this problem by never asking any friend to do anything for them (they call asking people to do things 'imposing'). To me, this is throwing the baby out with the bathwater. It is better to make sure you have two-way traffic. Chapter 8 explains how.

A word about money and one-way traffic. The subject of paying people to do things is covered in full in Chapter 10. But it is worth mentioning here that money entitles you to one-way traffic. Mrs B cleans your house for you. You don't clean hers. But you pay her. You do your boss's typing. She doesn't do yours. But she pays you. The great danger is that this legitimate one-way traffic flows over into unrelated and inappropriate areas. You expect Mrs B to listen to your troubles. Do you listen to hers? Your boss expects you to drive her home after the office party. Does she return the compliment? Remember: paying someone entitles you to get them to do those things specified in their contract, written or unwritten. It does not entitle you to permanent one-way traffic.

Resentment

Resentment ruins relationships. 'One-way traffic' of the kind just described, and unbalanced traffic, where most of the telling is done by one party, lead to resentment. Resentment is pernicious, because often we appear to be being successful in our endeavours to get people to do things; only later do we discover that we have stoked an enormous smouldering fire of resentment in the process.

Again, fear of arousing resentment leads many of us to avoid all but the most carefully thought-out exchanges of help. Yet it is better to learn how to create conditions which control and cure resentment. The next two chapters provide some advice.

Loss of control

If you do something yourself, you can control precisely when and how it is done. Your control is always less when you get someone else to do it. Many bosses find it incredibly difficult to delegate – they know they could 'do it better' themselves. Some mothers find it hard to let their children clean their own teeth, brush their hair, tidy up their toys – they could certainly do it better, and faster, themselves. Some people solve their anxiety over loss of control by 'hovering' when they get someone else to do a job. They can hardly bear to let them out of their sight.

This is *not* the way. We all have to accept that others will do things differently from us – maybe better, maybe worse, but always differently. Chapter 9 looks at how we can have some control over the product of what we get others to do; but that control cannot be complete – nor should we want it to be. One of the most important reasons for getting other people to do things is that they will certainly bring new skills, new approaches, new ideas to the task.

So, properly understood, 'loss of control' is not in fact a pitfall, but a benefit.

The benefits of getting other people to do things

There are several other fundamental benefits of getting others to do things rather than doing everything ourselves. I shall discuss these under four headings: lack of skill, lack of will, lack of distance, and desire to build. When any one of the conditions summarized by each heading prevails, then it is time to get someone else to do the job.

Lack of skill

No-one can be competent at everything. Maybe once, hundreds of thousands of years ago, man was a solitary animal, catering for all his own needs. But in our highly developed, technologically based society, we simply can't in one lifetime acquire all the skills we need to survive and, more importantly, make the most of life.

As a quick exercise, write down every machine or device you use in the course of a day. Now tick the ones you could mend if they went wrong – probably hardly any of them. It just goes to show how dependent we are on other people to do things for us.

Some people find this dependence difficult to bear. They think they ought to be able to do everything themselves, that it's somehow weak or lazy to ask someone else. Well, the time is long since gone when we even had a choice in the matter. Often people can easily recognize that they need doctors and dentists, plumbers and electricians, specialists of all kinds, but they have difficulty accepting that other ordinary people might also be an important resource, and a resource that they should use. If you are one of these people, if you are the sort someone might refer to as 'fiercely independent', just think back to Chapter 2 of this book, and to the section entitled, 'Know your strengths'. We said then that your strengths might be many and varied, that they might not have a standard label attached such as 'linguist' or 'mathematician' but they might be qualities like persistence or humour. Well, the same is true for everyone else. There are all sorts of resources in others just waiting to be tapped, even if they have no letters after their name and no certificates on their walls.

Lack of will

There are lots of things we could do but don't want to. Sometimes our puritanical forefathers whisper in our ear: 'Never mind if you don't want to do it; it's wrong to get someone else to do something you *could* do yourself.'

Cast your mind back to 'Working out why' in the KR–3W plan (Chapter 2). We said then that if you don't have a good reason for doing something, it's better not to begin. Find someone else to do it.

If you're not motivated, it will take you longer and you won't do it so well.

If you can't find someone else (or you can't afford them when you've found them!), then of course you may have to do the job yourself. But where there's lack of will, it's always worth investigating the alternatives. After all, if you find out you're absolutely the only person to clear out the shed/write to the American aunt/ telephone those potential clients, then that in itself may motivate you sufficiently to achieve.

Lack of distance

Sometimes we are too close to a problem, *too* anxious about the result, too heavily committed, to do what needs to be done. Many behavioural and learning problems in young children need to be handled primarily by outsiders, not by the parents. The parents are so close to the problem, they're part of it. They must ask someone else to help their child.

It is partly for this reason, 'lack of distance', that teachers are not encouraged to teach their own children, nor solicitors to provide legal services to their own families, and doctors are forbidden by law from treating their relatives. Lack of distance is a particularly relevant consideration when feelings are likely to run high, but it can be significant in other situations too. I know an expert carpenter who never does any carpentry in his own home. It isn't that he hasn't the time or doesn't want to; he finds that the work he does at home is never good enough for him. He notices slight flaws and imperfections, and he can't enjoy what he has produced. He is quite happy with someone else's handiwork, though, and doesn't subject it to the same unreasonable scrutiny.

Desire to build

This is the single most important reason for getting other people to do things. Friendships, businesses, families, groups of all kinds, depend on people being able to get each other to do things. And if you want to build a stronger team, a closer family, a more committed friendship, then you need to do things – with others, for others and, just as importantly, through others.

'Desire to build' is relevant in another sense too. The best way to build someone else's skills and confidence, is to get them to do things themselves.

The do-it-yourself quiz

Having made the case for getting other people to do things, we finish this chapter with a quiz to find out how much you do just that. Choose an answer for each question, and the points you get are given in brackets after the answer.

1. Do you pay anyone to do any work in your home (housework, babysitting, plumbing etc.)?
   - (a)   Yes   (0)
   - (b)   No   (10)
2. When was the last time you asked someone's advice?
   - (a)   You never do   (10)
   - (b)   In the last few days   (5)
   - (c)   In the last few minutes   (0)
3. Which of these adjectives best fits you?
   - (a)   Independent   (10)
   - (b)   Sharing   (5)
   - (c)   Leaning   (0)
4. At work, do you have anyone working directly to you?
   - (a)   Yes – several people   (0)
   - (b)   Yes – onc or two people   (5)
   - (c)   No   (10)
   - (d)   Irrelevant; I don't go to work   (5)
5. You have cut your finger badly. Would your first instinct be to:
   - (a)   Phone for an ambulance   (−5)
   - (b)   Scream   (0)
   - (c)   Run it under cold water, and dress it yourself   (10)

If you scored 0 or below, you are so dependent on other people you had better read the rest of this book quickly before your life support system wears out.

If you scored over 40, you are so independent you had better read the rest of this book to find out what it means to belong to the human race.

Otherwise, read on anyway – you'll probably find it interesting.

8

Asking People to Do Things

Motivation or manipulation?

Peter Machiavelli ran a small software consultancy. One day he called one of his promising young software designers into his office and spoke to her along the following lines.

You're doing extremely well, and I'm very pleased with your progress. In fact, I think it's time you had some broader experience of the company and its clients, and I've seen the ideal opportunity for you. My Marketing Director needs an assistant, to help him conduct visits with potential clients, respond to invitations to bid for work, and generally get the company known. That position would be just right for you at this stage of your career, and so we'd like to offer it to you before we advertise for someone from outside. You're inexperienced in this area, but we feel you would learn fast – and we want to demonstrate to you in the most concrete terms that we're committed to seeing you progress and develop. How about it?

What Peter Machiavelli did not tell this young employee was that the Marketing Director was very difficult to work with, that the company feared they would not find anyone prepared to put up with him and that one of the main reasons she had been chosen to fill the position of his assistant was that she was attractive, well spoken and very popular with clients. In other words, he had presented the offer entirely as something *she* needed, whereas it was in reality a response to the *company's* needs.

I suspect that the people reading this story will react in one of two ways. Some will think: 'What a clever bit of footwork by Peter Machiavelli. He'll solve his problems and make his employee feel good at the same time.' Others, on the other hand, will think: 'How dishonest! That's no way to run a company!'

Before I tell you what I think, let's consider how else Peter

Machiavelli might have presented the offer to his employee. Let us suppose he spoke to her on these lines.

> You're doing extremely well, and I'm very pleased with your progress. In fact, I've got sufficient confidence in you to wonder if you can help us out with a bit of a tricky problem. My Marketing Director needs an assistant. In a lot of ways you'd be ideal – you're personable, the clients like you, you pick things up quickly. True, you'd have quite a bit to learn, but I don't think that would be a problem. The difficulty is though that our Marketing Director is brilliant with clients but not easy to work with. I think we'd have to sort out exactly how you and he would work together, perhaps give you clearly demarcated lines of responsibility and so on, otherwise you might find it all a bit tricky. On the other hand, you could regard it as a challenge, and you would certainly gain a lot of very useful knowledge across the company. What do you feel?

Let me put my cards on the table now, and say that I consider the way Peter Machiavelli actually did handle this interview with his young employee to be manipulative. It would have been far better had he motivated her in the more honest way we have just imagined. Why better that way? Why is it better to motivate than to manipulate? What is the difference anyway?

Let's just consider some of the dangers in Machiavelli's approach.

1. He is hiding the fact that the Marketing Director is known to be difficult to work with. Such facts have an uncanny habit of coming to the surface. When his employee finds out, she will be angry, disappointed and may feel used. She may leave the company.
2. The kind of relationship Machiavelli is fostering with his employees is one where he holds all the cards. They are pawns in his game. Pawns rarely realize their full potential; they are limited because their understanding of what is going on is limited. Had he been open with his young employee, Machiavelli might have tapped her resources of tact and determination; as it is, she will go into the new situation unprepared and problems will almost certainly follow.
3. If Machiavelli manipulates his employees, they will consider it

fair game to manipulate him. For example, instead of asking him for time off, they will pretend to be sick. Instead of telling him they are considering leaving, they will appear absolutely committed until the point at which they hand in their notice (with a smirk!)

4. Maybe Machiavelli's approach motivates his employee better in the short-term. She feels grateful, enthusiastic, buoyant. But she will rapidly become demotivated when she discovers the realities of the situation. And if she blames herself for the problems, she will lose heart even more. Her work will deteriorate, and Machiavelli's profits will suffer.

There is an important difference between *motivating* people and *manipulating* them. When you motivate people to do things, you consider what's in it for *them*, you put yourself in their shoes, and you present your request in the light of those thoughts. When you manipulate them, you consider only what's in it for *you*, and how you can get what you want.

Although the example above is drawn from a work environment, understanding the difference between motivating and manipulating people is even more important when asking family and friends to do things. Because with them you want to build and keep longlasting relationships, based on trust and mutual respect. If you want your son to help with the washing-up, is it better to say, manipulatively, 'I've got a terrible headache, I think I must lie down' or to motivate him by saying, 'Everytime you do the washing-up, I'll give you 20p'? If you want your friends to help out more with the journeys to and from school, will you manipulate them by complaining in a general fashion about wear and tear on your car, or will you say, 'Let's draw up a rota for the school run, and find out which days are best and worst for each of us?' Often it is easier to manipulate, because you don't have to be honest about what you're doing, but manipulation stores up problems for the future and leaves a nasty taste for most of us.

How to avoid manipulating: twenty don'ts

1. Don't pretend you're helping someone when you're asking them to help you.

2. Don't hide what's in it for you.
3. Don't give them a carefully laundered account.
4. Don't feign illness or weakness.
5. Don't imply that the person you're asking is unkind or weak if they say 'no'.
6. Don't suggest your friendship hangs on their saying 'yes'.
7. Don't feel smug (Feeling smug is a warning sign!).
8. Don't avoid eye contact.
9. Don't flatter to 'soften them up'.
10. Don't threaten.
11. Don't even hint at unpleasant things that might happen if they say no.
12. Don't conceal consequences.
13. Don't conceal difficulties in the job.
14. Don't say, 'Personally I wouldn't have asked you, but X insisted.'
15. Don't start with, 'I've never asked anything of you before, but. . . .'
16. Don't say, 'It's only a small thing', when it isn't.
17. Don't play on the fears and/or hopes of the person you're asking.
18. Don't pretend you're indifferent when you're not — 'I don't mind one way or the other. . . .'
19. Don't rush people unnecessarily — 'I need to know right now.'
20. Don't imagine you're more important than you are.

A better way: potted guide to assertiveness

What is assertiveness?

This chapter has started off with how *not* to ask people to do things. We need to look more closely at how *to* do it, now, and that is where assertiveness comes in. In a nutshell, assertiveness is to do with standing up for your own rights while respecting those of other people. It is different from aggressiveness, which is to do with standing up for your own rights to the exclusion of other people's, and from submissiveness, which is failing to stand up for your rights.

Assertiveness is relevant to many many areas of life, both at work and at home. Here we are going to consider it just in relation to asking other people to do things. You can replace the twenty 'don'ts' in the previous section with one 'do':

> If you don't want to be manipulative, be assertive!

Rights

I am not about to debate the vexed and deep question of whether people have 'basic human rights' and what these might be. All we need to accept to be assertive is that people have *equal* rights. If I have a right to ask you to do something, then you have a right to ask me to do something. If I have a right to ask, you have a right to say no.

This is a truly liberating notion. A lot of people find it difficult to assert their rights because they feel to do so would be to oppress others. This often lies behind the 'martyr mentality' – someone who spends his or her life at other people's beck and call. Yet once we understand that rights are like Newton's actions and reactions – every right has an equal and opposite counter-right – we are free to use our rights, knowing that this makes those around us free to use theirs.

Let me illustrate this with a simple example. Suppose I want to ask my home help to clean the windows. I'm worried, because it hasn't been part of her duties so far, and it might be asking too much. So I don't ask her.

But if I recognize that she has the right to say 'no', I am free to ask her. She might like the variety of cleaning windows, or she might consider it too strenuous. In any event, once I've asked, she can decide whether or not to agree.

Imagine people saying 'no'

For reasons that are rooted in universal human fears of rejection and abandonment, we don't like to hear people saying 'no.' And so we get into the habit of only asking when we expect people to say 'yes'. And from there it's a small step to being affronted when people do say 'no'.

In order to be able to get other people to do things, we must get right out of this destructive position. The best way of achieving this is

84

to imagine other people saying 'no', even before we ask them, to bring it home to ourselves that their saying 'no' is a real and acceptable possibility.

Suppose you want to ask your next-door neighbour to water your garden while you are away. Imagine the conversation. Think of yourself posing the question. Then think of him saying, 'I'm sorry, but I've got such a lot on at work at the moment I don't feel I can do it.' What will you say then? How will you feel? What alternative arrangements can you make?

If you are asking someone to do something, you should not be totally dependent on their saying 'yes'. Remember: they have the right to say 'no'.

How to say 'thankyou'

Since people have the right to say 'no', it's important to thank them when they say 'yes'. After all, they've agreed willingly – they haven't been manipulated or coerced.

It's surprising how difficult it can be to say 'thankyou'. I think this is partly because we fear it puts us in the other person's debt, and partly because we fear it might sound patronizing. So when you say 'thankyou', think to yourself that it is shorthand for, 'I am grateful that you freely agreed to do what I asked, and that our equal relationship can continue. You may ask me to do things for you in the future, and I shall, like you, be free to say "yes" or "no".'

A bit of a mouthful, but it may help.

Being clear

So far we have been discussing the right *attitude* for asking other people to do things. After all, if your attitude isn't right, you might as well not ask at all, because you will find it's more trouble than it's worth.

Now we turn our attention to how we make sure people really understand what we are asking of them. Whenever two people meet, two worlds meet. Each of us brings with us a huge suitcase full of past experiences, expectations, hopes, fears and preconceptions. So the following kinds of communications happen.

1. *Boss says:*   Would you attend this meeting with me?

85

Employee hears:	Would you have an affair with me?
or:	Would you like to be promoted soon?
or:	When are you going to be reliable enough to go to meetings on your own?

When the employee says 'yes', he or she will be intending to do quite different things in each case!

2. | *Husband says*: | Would you iron this shirt for me? |
Wife hears:	Would you be more of a conventional wife?
or:	Would you make allowances for me because I'm tired?
or:	Would you help me feel confident for this important meeting tomorrow?

And so on and so on.

Given this universal characteristic of human communication, it's somewhat amazing that any of us ever manages to ask someone else to do something.

'Oh no', I can hear you groan. 'She's going to tell us we have to spell everything out, write everything down, cover all the options and be completely unambiguous when we ask people to do things. It'll be so time-consuming and tedious.'

Well, you'll be relieved to know that I'm not. That is the route for computers. We are human beings, and constitutionally incapable of that kind of robot-like clarity.

There is one simple way to ensure clarity in your requests. Because you are not seeking objective or scientific clarity: you are seeking *communication* clarity. And that communication is between two human beings. So those two are the only people who matter. As long as they understand each other, that's fine.

The simple rule is: think about where they're coming from. Put yourself in their place, try to imagine what their suitcase holds. More specifically, run through the following questions in your head:

- What kind of relationship do we have at the moment?
- What are his or her particular concerns at the moment?
- Have I ever asked him or her to do anything like this before?

It needn't take long, but this sort of imagination is worth its weight in gold, in terms of avoiding misunderstanding. Think about not only what you will ask of someone, but what they will hear you ask.

Some other useful reminders

Whilst the rule above is the most fundamental to being clear and making yourself understood, it is worthwhile just running through this clarity checklist for particularly important or complex requests.

- Is the timescale clear?
- Is the allocation of responsibility clear?
- How will we know when it's been done?
- Are the limits clear?
- Is the objective clear?

Here are some examples of 'unclear' requests. At which point in the clarity checklist does each fall down?

- Shall we tidy up the garage this afternoon?
- Would you collect Pete from school?
- Would you take over this project?

People who misunderstand on purpose

If you have thought about where he is coming from, you will probably have identified the person who misunderstands on purpose in advance. You then have two options.

1. Cut your losses. Trying to get this kind of person to do things is exhausting and unrewarding.
2. Solve the fundamental problem of why he wants to misunderstand. Perhaps he feels you always get your own way and there is no other means by which he can have some freedom; perhaps he thinks you are not entitled to ask him to do things.

You may be surprised that I have not included an option to be totally clear, write everything down, and make sure misunderstanding is impossible. That is because I think the notion that you can ask someone to do something in an infallibly precise way is a fantasy. If they want to misunderstand, they will find a way.

The skilful asker

When we call to mind people we know, at home and at work, some stand out in our minds as being particularly successful at asking people to do things. They are seldom misunderstood, never resented; other people actually seem to like it when they ask them to do things. They aren't bossy, yet they get an enormous amount done through other people.

Maybe we can identify some characteristics of the 'skilful asker'.

- He (or she) is genuinely interested in the people he asks to do things.
- He makes them feel excited about what they have been asked to do.
- His approval and attention are worth having.
- He is genuinely interested in the outcome of the task he's asking someone to do.
- He is prepared for others to say 'no' and doesn't bear grudges.
- He listens as well as asks.
- He sees others as colleagues and friends, not as tools and workers.

I think this can be summed up in the phrase, 'Those who give, get.' If you want to be successful at asking people to do things, make sure you do something for them.

9

Keeping People Going

Remember Chapter 6, about keeping yourself going until you finish the job? Well, when you have asked someone else to do something for you, you need to consider how you will keep *them* going.

If you have asked in an assertive way and received the answer 'yes', if you have put yourself in their shoes when explaining what you want done, then you will already have gone a long way towards ensuring the job gets done. However, more is necessary, if you really want people to do their best for you.

The importance of feedback

Imagine a good friend of yours has asked you to decorate his house. He is paying you, and you are pleased to have the work, since you are currently unemployed. He has asked you to do it while he's away on a fortnight's holiday, so that you have free run of the house and he isn't inconvenienced more than necessary.

You start work on the first day with enthusiasm. You get a lot done, much more than you expected. You take a pride in doing a good job, and paint along the skirting boards and round the electric points with great care.

By the third day, the job is becoming rather tedious. You've started to be less meticulous about painting in dark corners, behind radiators, and between bookshelves. The longer the job goes on, the slower you are, and by the end of the fortnight you have resolved never to take anything like this on again.

Now imagine your friend did not go on holiday for the fortnight you were painting his house. Every evening, he came back home from work, and saw what you had accomplished that day. He was particularly impressed by the neatness of the job, and said so. At the end of the third day, when you'd painted the hall, he was so pleased with the effect he opened a bottle of wine for you both to have at supper. You had every evening meal together, and talked about colour schemes in the light of what had been achieved to date.

I hardly need to point out that in the second story you would work harder, do a better job, and enjoy it more. And the reason for all of that? Feedback.

Notice that in neither of the two scenarios I drew was criticism involved. In fact, criticism is vastly overrated as a means of getting people to achieve more, better, faster. The key difference between the first and second was *contact* between you and the person you were working for, together with lots of interest on his part in what you were doing.

'Well', I can hear you say, 'this is all pretty obvious. Of course people won't do a good job unless you give them feedback.'

To make sure you're doing just that with those you have asked to do things, answer the following five questions.

1. Think of a situation where someone was doing some work for you in your home (cleaner, plumber, carpenter, builder, etc.). Did you make a point of being around or did you leave them to it?
2. There are no doubt some things you always ask others to do for you, because you can't do them yourself (for example, service your car, do your accounts, mend your TV). Do you know a certain amount about each of these areas, so that you can show an 'intelligent interest' in what is being done?
3. Do you ask your doctor and your dentist to explain why they are doing what they are doing?
4. Do you ever engage waitresses, shop assistants and garage attendants in conversation?
5. Do you know who cleans the office you work in? Would you recognize them in the street? Would you smile and say hello?

You may realize, having answered these questions, that you are giving an impression of indifference to some of the people you in fact rely on to do things well for you. Very few of us give enough feedback. Yet if we're not interested in what's being done, neither will they be, no matter how large a cheque we pay them at the end of the job.

Different kinds of feedback

Personal contact and personal interest are the best sources of feedback for people who are doing things for us. I always made a point of taking the manuscript of my first book round to the lady who typed it for me, although it would have been easier to post it. She was elderly and lived alone; it was particularly important both to me and to her that the work she did for me, although paid for, was done in the context of a friendship, of mutual interest and concern.

It is not, however, always possible, or necessary, to give feedback through personal contact. Here are four alternative feedback mechanisms that you could use, and how you might use them.

1. *'Chunk the job'* Split the job into smaller bits. Payment, or thanks, or details of the next bit, come at the end of each 'chunk' –and constitute the feedback.
2. *Leave notes* If you never see your cleaning lady/washing machine repair man/childminder – leave notes; make them personal and maybe amusing. You know it's working well when they write you notes back!
3. *Use the results of their labours* This is often the most satisfying feedback of all for someone who is working for you. Imagine a firm is laying a carpet throughout your house. On the evening of the first day, when you get in from work, they have completed the sitting-room. Why not arrange the furniture there, so that the next day, when the men return to lay the rest, they can literally *see* how pleased and enthusiastic you are with their achievement.
4. *Arrange feedback through an 'ambassador'* When my garden patio was being laid, I didn't see the men doing the work at all, because it was dark before I got back from work and they had long since gone home. My six-year-old son happened to be off school with a bad cold at the time, however, and he spent a lot of time in the garden, 'helping' the men and talking about how the garden was changing. Clearly, he was not supervising them in any formal sense, yet I'm sure he was a very effective motivator! Similarly, neighbours who look over the fence and say, 'My, that's a good job,' can be worth their weight in gold.

The hidden message

There is a crucial element in motivating others which has been implied in this discussion of feedback but which needs to be made explicit. It has to do with making a task part of a relationship rather than an arid, mechanical thing. It explains why people have the potential to be good leaders while computers, no matter how sophisticated, do not.

When someone is doing a job of work for you, make yourself a real person to him. Tell him why you want it done; talk to him about your best hopes and worst fears for the job; tell stories of previous successful and unsuccessful attempts to get it done. Then, as he works, his work will have meaning. It will be set in the context of a relationship. It will be to do with improving someone else's quality of life.

Incidentally, not only will this approach keep people going when they might otherwise have given up. It will also make it much more difficult for them to cheat or deceive you.

Managing commitment

If you give people no feedback, they will become demotivated and either give up or do less. If you are overinvolved with how and what they are doing, however, you run the risk of taking away from them the responsibility for success and achievement. And, when you're getting other people to do things, that is disastrous.

Let us illustrate this problem by taking a situation to extremes. Imagine you have asked someone to write a letter. Here is a set of ways you can get her to do it.

- You guide her hand over the paper, essentially writing the words for her.
- You dictate the letter; she writes.
- You give her the topics to be covered; she writes the letter, you review it.
- You tell her the objective of the letter; she writes it, you review it.
- You tell her the general subject matter; she writes and sends it.

What is varying in this sea of possibilities is the degree of control you have over the contents of the letter and, in direct inverse proportion, the degree of commitment she has to the quality of that letter. You cannot have high control *over* someone and high commitment *from* them. As their own creativity is engaged so their commitment increases. Take away their room for manoeuvre, and their commitment nosedives.

It doesn't matter if you threaten the letter writer with dire punishments if the letter isn't good, or promise her massive pay rises if it's excellent: such 'extrinsic' punishments and rewards will only make her committed to avoiding or obtaining these punishments and rewards, *not* to producing a good letter.

To get the best from people, over time, you must manage their commitment. This means identifying what they are good at and allowing them the freedom to use their skills.

Five years ago, a friend of mine had to choose an architect to design a house for him. He was himself good at visualizing buildings and spaces; and he had some quite precise ideas about what he wanted. But he went to considerable trouble to find an architect who had already designed houses he liked. This was not just because such an architect would be more skilled at doing what he, my friend, wanted, but more importantly because he could give such an architect some freedom in deciding the design. And that way he would be more committed, and enthusiastic, and do a better job.

The guiding principle is: find the best you can (and can afford) and give him or her as much freedom as you can.

Now clearly in many situations you cannot take the risk of losing control. You might end up with a beautifully decorated living-room, in a colour you cannot stand, for example! So each time you get someone else to do something, you need to find the right balance of control and commitment (*and* feedback). People vary in how much feedback they need, how much control they can tolerate, and how hard you have to work to enlist their commitment. Here are some warning signs that you haven't got the balance right:

- Things are left half-done, for you to complete (too little commitment).
- Only things you have specifically asked for get done, no extras, no 'value-added' (too little commitment).
- The person or people working for you start avoiding you (too much control).
- They ask you to make decisions on every aspect of the task, no matter how trivial (too little commitment).
- There are lots of mistakes, which could certainly have been avoided (too little commitment).
- Misunderstandings arise (too little control).

- The 'working day' becomes shorter and shorter (too little commitment).
- You find things finished but in a way you would not have chosen (too little control).
- The pace of work is slow (too little commitment).

I would say that many more problems in keeping people going derive from too little commitment than from too little control. To increase someone else's commitment, try the following:

- Ask them what they think.
- 'Back off' – arrange to be too busy or away for a while (that is, decrease *your* commitment – theirs will often increase in response).
- Acknowledge ignorance about some aspect of the task.
- Acknowledge the job is difficult/boring/taking longer than you had estimated.
- Give them a break.
- Put them more 'in charge' of what is done.
- Invest in the relationship – take them out for a meal, talk about other things than the job with them.
- Claim to feel uncommitted yourself.

Note Painting a rosy picture of the benefits of completing the task, in effect, 'selling it', is often the *worst* thing you can do if someone's commitment is low. You continue to be the one who really cares about it, leaving them free to be irresponsible.

10

Paying People to Do Things

Money and embarrassment

There is something about money changing hands which causes us
problems. Just pause for a minute and picture yourself in the
following situations.

- negotiating the price of a piece of pottery with the potter who
  made it
- asking a neighbour to pay back a small amount of money you lent
  her a few days ago
- discussing how much you should be paid for a job you are going to
  do for someone

How did you feel when you pictured yourself in these scenarios? I
would not be at all surprised if one of your feelings was embarrassment, combined with a desire to avoid talking about money, to
escape from these rather uncomfortable tasks.

Don't imagine it is because you aren't used to these kinds of
exchanges that you felt embarrassed. Salesmen have to undergo
lengthy training to overcome the embarrassment and diffidence they
naturally feel about trying to get a good price. Many professional
people find it well-nigh impossible to be 'upfront' about what they
are going to charge for their services and pay someone else to deal
with all that. It is a common human experience: money changing
hands is embarrassing. Somehow when we ask for money we are
asking for evidence that we are valued; when we pay money, we are
terrified that we will undervalue the recipient.

The solution to this is not to run away from financial transactions
(as many people do). It is to confront what is involved, to be clear
about why money is changing hands, and to be as straightforward
and fair as we can in deciding how much, what for and when. This
chapter is about achieving these objectives. And the first step is to
put money firmly in its place, to be clear about what it can and can't
buy.

What money can buy

There are two main things money can buy with respect to getting things done: skill, and time. If you don't have the expertise or specialist qualification to do a job, or to do it well enough, you can pay someone who has. Similarly, if you don't have the time, or the inclination to spend your time that way, you can buy some of someone else's.

We all find it relatively easy to accept that money can be used to buy skill. After all, the decision to pay is often made for us. Even if we wanted to, we wouldn't be able to represent ourselves in court, fill our own teeth, or put our own car through an MOT.

But many of us find it extremely difficult to use money to buy *time*. We are so used to thinking that our own time is 'free', and we so often have unrealistic expectations about what we can achieve ourselves (see Chapter 2!) that we aren't really convinced that 'buying time' is ever justified.

Yet time is the only thing that really matters. Time to relax, to enjoy ourselves, to get to know each other better, to achieve what we are best at achieving. If you have never bought anyone else's time before, try it just once, in a small way, and see how it can add to your life. Maybe the garage needs tidying up and clearing out. Ask two reliable teenagers to do it for you in return for a reasonable fee. Then, while they are doing it, relish the fact that the time you have then is extra. You have bought it. Sometimes we ourselves achieve twice as much in time we have bought than in any other kind of time; then buying time is really cost-effective!

Conversely, make sure you don't buy time without realizing it. When you hire a babysitter, you're buying time. So let's hope that what you do with the time you've bought is worth it!

What money can't buy

There are two things we often think, or hope, money will buy which it never will. You may already know which two I am thinking of from reading the last chapter. They are: commitment, and freedom from responsibility.

In fact, paying people to do things, interestingly enough, tends to discourage 'commitment' because it often leads to the attitude, 'I'm only doing this for the money'. Similarly, if you are paying, then you have an *additional* responsibility rather than freedom from responsibility: to make sure you are getting value for money.

So don't make the fatal mistake of thinking that because you are paying someone else to paint your house, manage your business, look after your child, you can forget all about it. Turn back to Chapter 9 and remind yourself of how you *do* ensure commitment and quality work.

So what are you buying?

When we go into a shop and buy a new drill, for example, we know exactly what we are buying. We see it, examine it, maybe even ask for a demonstration of how it works, before we hand over the money. What You See Is What You Get ('WYSIWYG' as the computer boffins say).

But when we pay someone to do something, we are in a totally different situation. At the time we agree the fee, we often have little idea what we will get in return. Suppose we ask a company to clean our house. Will they wash down grubby paintwork? Will they vacuum under loaded bookshelves? Will they polish the wooden furniture? We don't find out until after they have finished and submitted their invoice.

It is not possible to specify to the last detail what you want someone to do, as we said in Chapter 8. On the other hand, to avoid disappointment, disagreements and disaster, you should ask yourself the following questions before you agree to pay someone.

- Is the timescale clear?
- Is the allocation of responsibility clear?
- How will we know when it's been done?
- Is the objective clear?

You may recognize these questions from Chapter 8. The reason why they're particularly important when you're paying someone to do something is that, as we have already discussed, when money is involved feelings run high and the consequences of misunderstanding are potentially more serious.

Also, being absolutely clear about what you're buying means you're more likely to get value for money.

Deciding how much to pay: right and wrong considerations

When you're deciding how much to pay someone, you need to consider the following:

- How much can you afford? (if you can't afford what it costs you can't go any further)
- How much is the job worth to you? (this is a separate question, which only you can answer)
- How much do other people pay for similar jobs? (it's surprising how often we neglect to research this essential question)
- How much an hour does the person you are thinking of employing normally get?

But you should *not* consider the following – which in fact often turn out to be determining factors when we decide how much to pay!

- Will I be embarrassed if I offer more/less than this (*Remember*: we must overcome embarrassment by being clear about what the money is for, not by throwing money at the problem!)
- Will other people be impressed if I pay more/less than this?
- How much does this person need? (charity and paid employment rarely mix well)

False economies

When paying other people to do things, we have to be particularly careful not to make false economies. One such is, of course, the well-known false economy of buying something cheap when what we really need is something expensive. (Putting the car through a local, 'we'll turn a blind eye', MOT when it really needs a thorough service would be an example of this.)

There are some false economies which apply specifically to paying people to do things. One is to beat the other's price down until he is doing the job for much less than he thinks is fair. He may do it, because he needs the money, but he will try to redress the balance by skimping on the job, so that in the end 'you get what you pay for' in his eyes.

Then there is the false economy of misleading someone about how long or how difficult a job is. Again, as soon as your deception comes to light, the top item on your employee's agenda will be how to mitigate the injustice done him. And if you pretend you didn't know, he will quite rightly expect you to offer to increase his fee. When you don't, you can wave farewell to the possibility of his doing a good job.

'Well', you may say, 'it's their lookout if they don't check what the job involves before agreeing the price. The law's on my side if they try to get their own back.'

Even if it is, do you really want to spend time and money in the courts? That rather destroys the point of getting someone else to do something in the first place, doesn't it? Unless, of course, you enjoy, as some do, lawsuits, court fights and exchange of angry letters.

The essential point is this: *any economy that results in loss of goodwill is false economy*. That doesn't mean you should be a sucker when you're paying. It is just as important that you are seen as someone who gets value for money as it is that you give fair money for value. None of us produces our best work for someone we don't respect.

Payment schedule

Let me introduce you to the 'power curve'. It describes the relationship between control, payment and time. It looks like this.

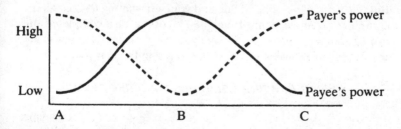

At point 'A', you (the 'payer') holds all the cards. The job is completed but you haven't paid yet. You've got what you want, and the 'payee' has no leverage (other than the courts, which, as we have already said, few in their right mind would want to refer to).

Then you pay the payee. Now the power relationship is reversed (point 'B'). The payee has what he wants. You are relatively powerless if you now find that the job he did is unsatisfactory or not what you really wanted after all.

As time goes by, the payee begins to wonder if you would employ him again. The power curve is gradually restored to its former pattern.

'What have all these curves to do with me?' I hear you ask. The management of these power curves will to a large extent determine the success of a job you ask someone else to do. The way to manage them is through payment schedules.

Whenever money changes hands, the balance of power shifts. The most productive relationships are those where power is never too unequally distributed. So just as you wouldn't dream of paying someone £100 000 in advance, so you should never allow someone to do £100 000 worth of work for you before you pay them anything. You need to determine a payment schedule which preserves the balance of power.

You may do this by paying in instalments, weekly or monthly. You may do it with stage payments, which are awarded as each part of a job is completed. You may pay, say, 70 per cent in instalments, and the last 30 per cent as a bonus at the end, to retain more power in your hands.

Obviously the kind of schedule on which you decide will depend on the length and size of the job, the relationship you want with the person you are paying, and expectations and previous experience. But one word of warning: if you find yourself wanting to keep all the cards, not to pay a cent until every last bit of the job is completed and inspected, then this could be a sign you don't trust your payee at all. So should you be asking him to do the job in the first place?

Special dangers when paying other people to do things

Causing offence

If you offer to pay someone who wants to give you their services for free, you may offend. If you offer too little, you may offend. If you offer too much, you may offend. Guard against this by doing your homework before you discuss money. How much is reasonable? What can you offer without implying you are superior/richer/in control? (You may like to refer to the 'Potted guide on assertiveness' in Chapter 8 for ideas on how to do this).

Loss of self-esteem

Many of us need to feel we are capable of spending money wisely in order to have self-respect. If we find we have been cheated, we can suffer a profound loss of self-esteem. We may feel of ourselves, 'I can't strike good deals. Other people can take advantage of me. I'm a sucker.' This is why it is so important to get the price right and to make sure you get value for money.

Illusion of control

Sometimes we imagine we can control someone else through money. We may delay or cut payment when they're not performing up to scratch, threaten to do so if they don't do exactly what we want, and hold out promises of extra rewards if they do really well. As Chapter 9 pointed out, you can't buy commitment or control. They have to be earned.

Conclusion

When we're faced with something we want to get done or, as is more usual, with a large number of things we want to get done, we often feel simply 'not up to it!'. It's as if there isn't enough inside us to do it.

This book has been about discovering how to tap the considerable resources we have inside us *and* about how to use extra resources *outside* of us. So now that you've read it, you can look at everything you have to get done in the light of those resources. It's no longer a question of not having enough, but of choosing the best. Where shall I do it? At what times? How shall I chunk the job? Shall I enlist other people's help? In what way? Shall I ask someone else to do it for me? Shall I pay him/her?

And the more experience you have of matching your resources to different jobs, the more confident and knowledgeable you will become about those resources. In short, you will become more and more resource-full, and resourcefulness is the key to effectiveness.